OTHER BOOKS BY TOM AINSLIE

THE COMPLEAT HORSEPLAYER

AINSLIE ON JOCKEYS

AINSLIE'S COMPLETE GUIDE TO THOROUGHBRED
  RACING

HANDICAPPER'S HANDBOOK

THEORY AND PRACTICE OF HANDICAPPING

AINSLIE'S COMPLETE GUIDE TO HARNESS RACING

AINSLIE'S COMPLETE HOYLE

AINSLIE'S ENCYCLOPEDIA OF THOROUGHBRED
  HANDICAPPING

HOW TO GAMBLE IN A CASINO

THE MOST FUN AT THE LEAST RISK

by TOM AINSLIE

GRAPHICS BY JADE FOREST DESIGN

A FIRESIDE BOOK
Published by Simon & Schuster
New York London Toronto Sydney Tokyo Singapore

Copyright © 1979 by Tom Ainslie
First Fireside Edition, 1987
Published by Simon & Schuster, Inc.

Rockefeller Center
1230 Avenue of the Americas
New York, New York 10020
Published by arrangement with the author.
Originally published in 1979 by William Morrow and Company, Inc.
FIRESIDE and colophon are registered trademarks of Simon & Schuster, Inc.
Designed by Carl Weiss
Manufactured in the United States of America
20   19   18   17   16   15   14   13   Pbk.
Library of Congress Cataloging-in-Publication Data

Ainslie, Tom.
    How to gamble in a casino.
    Reprint. Originally published : New York : Morrow,
1979.
    "A Fireside book."
    Bibliography: p.
    Includes index.
    1. Gambling. 2. Gambling systems. I. Title.
[GV1301.A37   1987]   795'.01   87-53
ISBN 0-671-63952-8 pbk.

CONTENTS

CONTENTS

9

CONTENTS

LIST OF ILLUSTRATIONS

INTRODUCTION:

LUCK AND SKILL IN GAMES OF CHANCE

AT THIS MOMENT, NUMEROUS CHEERFUL SOULS ARE WIN-
ning money in gambling casinos on five of the world's
continents. Their good fortune is entirely consistent with
the probabilities that govern the games they play. Before
you reach the bottom of this page, however, many of these
winners will become losers, having made foolish bets. They
should mend their ways. This book tells how.

Mine is by no means the first attempt to equip a fun-
loving public with the simple principles and techniques
that separate competent gamblers from the inept majority.
Dozens of experts, including scholars of great renown,
have written about casino play, dissecting the odds of each
game and analyzing the weaknesses of betting systems.
Other books have described and explained the theory of
probability or have reviewed what little is known about the
psychology of gambling. The literature is not only well-
intentioned. It is authoritative. But hardly anyone seems
to get the message. The typical casino gambler continues
to play badly, as if uninformed.

What we have here is a communications gap. I propose

to bridge it by addressing the audience in its own terms. I assume that the reader would like to know how to play casino games for maximum fun at minimum risk. I assume also that the reader wants easy and rapid access to the knowledge on which smart play depends. Accordingly, I submit a totally reader-oriented book, which delivers its message without algebraic equations, ancient history, reminiscences of the author's exploits, or other obstacles to clear communication.

After identifying certain basic realities of which the gambling public needs to be aware, I shall direct the reader to the specific games, bets, and money-management plans that furnish the best opportunities for gainful play. In reviewing those strategies, I shall offer approaches graded to the personality and ability of the individual. Persons unaccustomed to the hullabaloo of Craps, the rapid confusions of Blackjack, or the intimidating rituals of Baccarat will learn simple procedures with which they can tend their wholesome instincts of self-preservation while gambling with greater acumen than is typical, sad to say, of most veterans.

As to the experienced gambler, that two-fisted plunger for whom no vacation is complete without a series of extended flings at the tables, I insist that it is never too late to learn survival techniques. Here is an introductory assurance: Anybody who heeds the advice in these pages will never go home broke.

I approach all this with a light heart. Our subject is nothing to be grim about. It is a uniquely exciting recreation, a luxurious sport in which losing costs no more than the individual chooses to spend. Still lightly, I deny the common assumption that every player should expect to lose. That belief, which misunderstands the laws of probability, is one reason for weird casino performances by otherwise intelligent persons who play stupidly—playing to lose and not to win. It so happens that the best way to avoid loss, or at least limit its cost, is to play to win. Furthermore, playing to win requires no great exertion.

Let me now hasten to add that, although winning is a real possibility from time to time, persons of sound mind do not go to casinos to solve their financial problems. Aside from the casino owners, their employees, and a diminishing handful of Blackjack sharks with abnormal abilities, nobody makes a living at the tables. Gamblers who claim to support themselves by beating casino games either lie through their teeth or are headed for expensive disappointment.

Having agreed on the recreational purpose of gambling, we now should dispose of its supernatural aspect. I refer to the mystery known as luck. The repeated calamities suffered by many gamblers are attributable to baseless notions about luck, often combined with equally mistaken suppositions about the relationship between luck and personal character. Save for certain dedicated spendthrifts whose addiction to defeat proclaims a need for psychotherapy, the vast majority of habitual losers simply do not know what luck and gambling are about. If they did, they would be better gamblers. They will do well to read on.

GAMBLING AND LUCK

The chief stock-in-trade of the casino is the game of pure chance, such as Craps, Baccarat, or Roulette. The players of these games wager on events that occur at random, totally beyond human foresight or influence. Although everyone at the table should know the full range of *possible* results before any roll of the dice or turn of the wheel, nobody knows what the actual outcome will be. For example, the dice must produce a number between 2 and 12 inclusive. Whoever guesses correctly and wins a bet has done so by accident. Which raises a question.

Do the dice show a favorable number *because* the player is lucky? Emphatically not. To cope with the challenges and temptations of casino play, it is essential to understand that no human attribute (including a real or imagined history of good or bad luck) has the slightest effect on the outcome of the next bet. A winner is lucky to have won, but luck was not the cause.

I am not splitting hairs or playing with words. Superstitions about the miraculous powers of luck defeat thousands of gamblers by blinding them to the realities of the games they play. A casino is a recreation center, not a temple of the occult. Nothing could be less supernatural than the percentages that rule the games. Most of these numbers have been known for centuries. In recent years, they have been hashed over in computer studies so exhaustive that, for all practical purposes, everything worth knowing has been discovered and documented. Persons who do not appreciate the probabilities, and regard them as somehow secondary to luck, take foolish risks which multiply their chances of grave loss.

To repeat a point made earlier, it is possible to win at the tables now and then. It actually is easy to win more table sessions than you lose. Knowledge of the odds and of productive betting plans has everything to do with it. Luck has nothing to do with it except, if you insist, in personal conclusions about good luck or bad—irrelevant appraisals that cannot be made until after the game is over. We shall view each game in that light and let luck take care of itself.

THE HOUSE PERCENTAGE AND SKILL

A casino is a business establishment. It enriches its proprietors by accepting bets on terms unfavorable to the bettors. Yon high roller may go home thousands of dollars ahead of the game but, as a class, Craps players lose. The same is true of all other casino pastimes. Individuals win but the clientele as a whole does not.

To see what happens, consider the person who enjoys betting on Red or Black at American Roulette. Like bets on Odd, Even, High, or Low, a winning bet on Red or a winning bet on Black pays even money—the player gets a dollar of profit for each dollar wagered. Although American Roulette is a grossly unfavorable game, players of Red (or Black) sometimes encounter winning streaks and, if they choose, walk away winners. Over the year, however, the casino beats Red bettors at the rate of 20 times for every 38 spins of the wheel. It beats Black bettors at the identical rate. The wheel contains only 18 red numbers but 20 non-red ones. And it has only 18 black numbers but 20 non-black ones. This construction is a long-term guarantee that the house eventually will take $20 from Red or Black bettors for each $18 that it pays them. The house's advantage (known in the trade as "vigorish") amounts to a robust 5.26 percent of the money bet on Red and Black. The percentage reaps millions for the casinos and assures ruin for any customer who tarries too long at the table.

How, then, does any Roulette player win? For the answer, let us imagine 1 million spins of the wheel—much less than two years of play at an average Nevada table. Although Red will bob up with predictable frequency during that period—about 47 percent (47.4%) of the time —the color will not appear *exactly* 18 times in *every* series of 38 spins. During some sequences of 38, Red may win

24 or 30 or more times. At other stages, accidentally and in full compliance with the laws of probability, it may lose more than 30 times in a series of 38 chances.

Even when Red actually appears a model 18 times in 38 turns, its winning patterns are sure to vary widely. A series of 18 successive Reds at the beginning of a sequence would be within the realm of probability, as would alternation of Red and non-Red for 38 spins, or patterns in which Red streaked for two or three or five or seven consecutive wins. In a long period of play, the variations are enormous. No matter what the possibility, it materializes sooner or later. And a winner is someone who happens to wager on a particular pattern when it occurs. Coincidences of that kind take place every day, every hour, and almost every minute. During a year, thousands of persons quit the table and go home winners. But the casino continues to grind out its percentage. No active casino operator has ever applied for food stamps.

If the long-range probabilities are inflexibly biased against the player, and if short-range possibilities are almost limitlessly varied, where does skill fit in?

Countless gamblers who know better than to trust blind luck regard skill as an effort to exploit certain well-established probabilities. The trouble is that they often choose the wrong ones. A typical example is the player who sits at a Roulette table waiting for Red or Black or Odd or Even or High or Low to show itself three times in succession. Pretend that Black has just obliged. The player immediately bets on Red, believing that the probabilities require an imminent win for that color. In other words, Red is "due." This concept, like others cherished by losers, appeals to old-fashioned common sense but draws no support from the laws of probability. It leads directly to defeat.

No gambling occurrence is ever "due," much less "overdue." Gambling implements like dice and wheels are inanimate objects without memories. Each turn or toss is completely independent of all that have preceded it and all that may follow it. As to a supposedly imminent appearance by Red, we have already noted that the long-range probabilities built into a 38-number American Roulette wheel guarantee that Red will win about $^{18}/_{38}$ or 47 percent of the time. This means that the chances of winning on the next spin are *always* about .47, and Red is never more "due" at one time than at any other, regardless of what may have happened during the previous half hour.

One need not be a mathematics fan to appreciate the simple arithmetic of winning streaks, losing streaks, and "overdue" events. The probability that Red will appear on the next turn of the wheel is .47. The probability that it will appear on both of the next two turns is $.47 \times .47 = .221$. The probability that it will win on each of three turns is $.47 \times .47 \times .47 = .104$. The probability that it will win on each of four is $.47 \times .47 \times .47 \times .47 = .049$. Make it .05—a 19–1 long shot! Notice, however, that before any individual turn in that series, the chances of an appearance by Red were always .47! Thus, the person who bets on Red after three, eight, or twelve successive Blacks is betting on a .47 chance. The same person might just as well place the chips on Black, for which the chances always are an identical .47.

As implied, the 19–1 odds against four successive Blacks or Reds are meaningful only if a player contemplates betting against such a pattern *before* it begins. Persons who wager on events considered "overdue"—betting that the so-called law of averages ordains the prompt termination of somebody else's winning streak—are practitioners of something called the Theory of the Maturity of Chances, or the Gambler's Fallacy. I have lingered over it because it needs to be stamped out and because our discussion of it brings us to the very crux of the kind of thinking that divides smart gamblers from chumps.

We have seen that each event at the table is independent of all others. We have seen that the probability of each *kind* of independent event is always the same. We have seen that these probabilities hold up in the long run but that short-term patterns cover an enormous range of possibilities. We have seen that someone who bets against the continuation of a winning streak has no statistical advantage over someone who bets that the streak will be prolonged. Equally important, we have seen that winning and losing streaks, like luck itself, cannot be identified until after the fact. This knowledge will fortify us when we set about trying to manage our money at the tables.

Faith in "overdue" occurrences is costlier than faith in the prolongation of streaks, although the chances of gain or loss are always identical on the next turn or toss. The reason for this is that someone who loses a bet that depends on the *continuation* of a streak is now finished with the streak and can look elsewhere for something to bet on. But the poor soul who bets on "overdue" events becomes more deeply involved as losses mount and the expected color or number fails to appear. Doubling the size of the bet after each loss, as so many of these players do, finally necessitates a huge wager that the casino refuses to accept. The player has collided with the house limit. This restriction on the maximum amounts accepted as bets differs from place to place and game to game. It is the casino's way of guaranteeing that the percentages of each game will remain fully operational, yielding dependable profits. It protects those profits against maniacs who might arrive at a table with millions of dollars, double their bets after each loss, and inevitably wipe out the bank.

Having exposed the Gambler's Fallacy as a conspicuous lack of skill, we now describe skill. It consists of:

1. Confining play to the least unfavorable bets, as set forth in the chapters that follow.

2. Managing money to best advantage by
   a. Imposing a limit on the amount one is willing to lose at each session and

b. Imposing a much lower limit on the winnings to be sought at each session and

c. Betting systematically, in accordance with one of the procedures explained in Chapter Two and

d. Leaving the tables as soon as winnings or losses reach the prescribed limit.

That does not sound like much, but there is no more. Anyone bright enough to navigate to a casino entrance and old enough to gain admittance is capable of adequate skill. No additional skills are permitted. Neither players nor casinos are allowed to exercise the kinds of techniques that might influence the outcome of the events on which bets are made. To tamper with the actual turn of the card, roll of the dice, or spin of the wheel would suppress pure chance and transform a gamble into a swindle. Loaded dice, electronically controlled wheels, and crooked dealing procedures are by no means unheard of. Neither are crooked players. But the reader is likely to frequent well-known resorts which conduct honest games and are merciless toward cheating dealers. Honest games earn the casinos ample revenues. Rumors of dishonesty are bad for business.

DEALING WITH THE DEALERS

Rules and procedures differ materially from place to place and are subject to periodic revision. Nobody need feel self-conscious about asking casino employees for guidance. Do not be afraid of being disdained as a come-lately boob. Be assured that the biggest boobs in casinos are not newcomers but free-spending veterans on whom casino personnel lavish every possible attention. In short, the employees are there to drum up trade, not drive it away. If courteous treatment is not forthcoming, pick up and play at another table. But if you like the dealer and win a little, demonstrate *savoir faire* and improve future relations by tipping, which we shall describe in connection with the games themselves.

GAMBLING FEVER

The concept of maximum fun at minimum risk is both unreal and unwelcome to persons whose gambling appetites can be satisfied only by hectic, boozy, nightlong sessions in which they match their "luck" against the pitiless percentages and vast resources of the casino. The best way to win is to quit when accident provides a modest, temporary advantage at the table. This approach also requires interruption of play when losses begin mounting—but before they get out of hand. Each of those tactics is at variance with the self-defeating but extremely common practice of trying to build moderate winnings into fortunes, or trying to overcome moderate losses by sending good money after bad.

I shall not challenge the right of individuals to abandon themselves to gambling fever. Or the right of casinos to exploit that ailment. But I dispute the notion that gambling fever is a natural state of mind. I insist that normal human beings have neither the need nor the desire to waste their time and money in all-out efforts to achieve physical, mental, and financial exhaustion at some casino. Most readers will find it much more fun to play in relatively short bursts of activity, quitting when the reasonable stop-loss or stop-win limit is reached, and resuming play later, when the spirit moves.

Finally, maximum fun and minimum hazard are achieved by gambling only when sober and alert. When boredom or fatigue set in, knock off.

USING THIS BOOK

Now that I have served up guiding generalities indispensable to carefree play at the tables, we shall scrutinize Roulette. It is not the best opportunity for profit (especially in the Western Hemisphere), but it is the least complicated and confusing of the major games. It is leisurely, elegant, and a good deal of fun. To most of us, it represents casino high life, Breaking the Bank at Monte Carlo, the whole glamorous fantasy. I would not consider visiting a casino without spending at least an hour at Roulette, unfavorable though its percentages are.

Most betting systems are designed for Roulette, even though applicable to other casino games. Our discussion of Roulette will lead to a chapter on money management and betting systems. We then will be well equipped to discuss the best casino games and the best ways to play them.

Experienced gamblers may have outgrown their curiosity about Roulette or may believe that they have nothing more to learn about its simplicities. So be it. I urge them not to miss the chapter on money management and betting systems. Having absorbed that material and, I hope, having found some food for thought in the chapters on Craps and/or Baccarat and/or Blackjack, they will enjoy themselves in dry-run play with the tables of random numbers in Appendix B. A few short exercises will sharpen their skills for the next big assault on the casino. By the time other readers reach Appendix B and its simulated bets, they will be no less ready for rehearsal. After that, it's off to Nevada or New Jersey or the Caribbean or London or Macao or wherever. None of us will ever strike awe into the heart of a casino operator. But, knowing how to survive at the tables, we shall play in comfort, unburdened by awe of our own.

ONE:
ROULETTE

IN THE STANDARD EUROPEAN VERSION OF THIS LEISURELY entertainment, the house awards itself as little as 1.35 percent of the players' money. So gentle a bite, plus comfortable seating, a civilized pace, and solemn encouragement by the casinos, makes European Roulette the all-time favorite of system enthusiasts. Using the rim of the table as a desk on which to mark their tally sheets (which sometimes are supplied by the house), they bet with deliberation, seeking significance in every outcome and having a fine old time, lose or win.

The American game is faster and the house enjoys an advantage of 5.26 percent on most bets. If it were not so pleasant to watch the wheel spin in its burnished wooden bowl and listen to the ball go pocketa-pocketa-pocketa, Nevada-Caribbean Roulette would be worth nobody's attention. As it is, the high American percentage repels

ROULETTE LAYOUT

0		00
1	2	3
4	5	6
7	8	9
10	11	12
13	14	15
16	17	18
19	20	21
22	23	24
25	26	27
28	29	30
31	32	33
34	35	36
2 to 1	2 to 1	2 to 1

enough customers to make the game much less popular
here than in the Old World. This is too bad. As we shall
see, some casinos are trying to make Roulette more attractive by lowering the house take on certain bets. European-
style wheels and table layouts are found in certain Nevada
establishments, but not many.

AMERICAN ROULETTE

THE LAYOUT AND PROCEDURES

The wheel contains 38 compartments, labeled 1 through
36, plus 0 and 00. The playing table displays those numbers in the pattern illustrated on page 36. After most of the
players place their bets on the layout on the playing table,
the dealer spins the wheel in one direction and propels the
ball in the other direction near the upper rim of the bowl.
Betting ends while the ball is still in flight. The number and
color of the compartment in which the ball comes to rest
determine the outcome of every bet.

Having found a place at the table, the player purchases
checks (chips) from a dealer (croupier). Although dime
chips are available in a few places, the usual rock-bottom
value is 25 cents and the minimum bet accepted at the table
may be no lower than four chips—one dollar. At a table of
that kind, the maximum bet is likely to be $250 or $500.
For gamblers too jaded for moderation, tables with higher

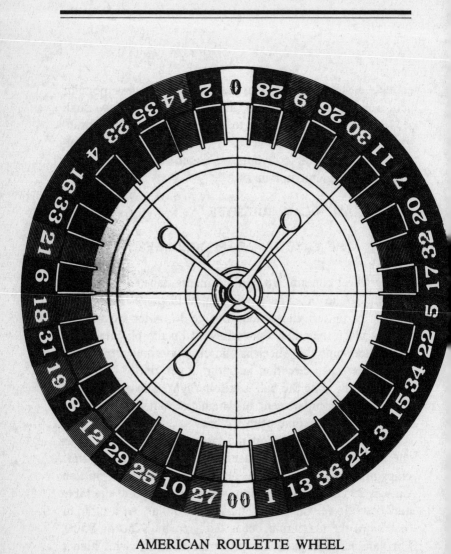

AMERICAN ROULETTE WHEEL

minimums and maximums are sure to be conveniently situated under the same roof.

Like all other casino games except Blackjack, Roulette is not as complicated as it first may seem. In fact, it is elementally simple. To make bets, one places chips on whatever part of the layout identifies the hoped-for outcome of the next turn of the wheel. If that part of the table is beyond easy reach, the croupier or an assistant will gladly place the chips in the desired location.

BETS AND ODDS

Save for one notably undesirable one (see "Five Numbers," below), all bets at American Roulette involve a house percentage of 5.26. This means that no bet is especially favorable. Here are the bets, and how to place them.

Straight: This is a bet on a single number—0 or 00 or anything from 1 through 36. To make the bet, one puts the chips in the correspondingly numbered area of the table. If the number wins, the croupier adds 35 chips to every chip that was bet. These odds of 35–1 are not high enough to compensate for the small chance that a particular number will appear on a given turn. The proper odds would be 37–1.

Split: To bet on two adjacent numbers at once, put the

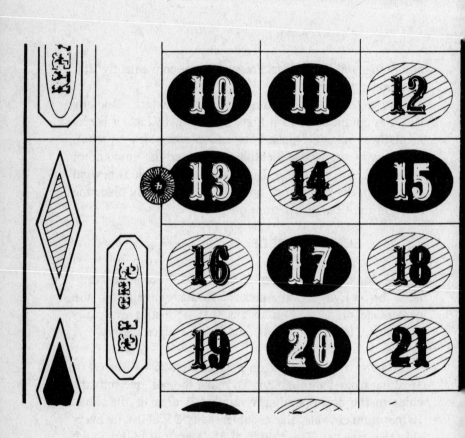

THREE-NUMBER BET

chips on the line that separates the numbers. If one of the numbers comes up, the house pays 17–1, and the vigorish remains the same 5.26 percent.

Three Numbers: Known as a *street* because it involves a bet on any three numbers that appear in a horizontal row on the layout. For example, 16, 17, 18. The bet pays 11–1 when one of the three numbers wins. Place the chips on the line (called the "sideline") that separates the nearest number of the desired street from the box labeled "1st 12," "2nd 12," or "3rd 12."

Corner: Known also as *Quarter*, this bet on any four adjoining numbers is made by putting chips on the intersection of the lines that separate the numbers from each other. When one of the numbers wins, the bet pays 8–1, maintaining the house percentage at 5.26.

Five Numbers: Sometimes called a *Five-Number Line*, this is a bet that the next turn will produce either 0, 00, 1, 2, or 3. It pays 6–1, which makes it the worst proposition on the board, with a house percentage of 7.89. The bet is made by putting chips at the intersection of the sideline and the line that separates the 0 from the 1.

Six Numbers: This kind of line bet is simply a play on two adjoining streets. The chips go where the sideline meets

SIX-NUMBER BET

the line separating the streets. If one of the numbers wins, the house pays 6–1, with the usual 5.26 percent vig.

Dozens: On the player's side of the sideline are boxes labeled "1st 12," "2nd 12," and "3rd 12," where chips are placed for bets, respectively, 1 through 12, 13 through 24, and 25 through 36. If the ball sticks on one of the selected dozen numbers, the player collects at the rate of 2–1.

Columns: At the extreme right of the layout are three boxes to receive bets on any of the three columns of 12 numbers each—1 through 34, 2 through 35, and 3 through 36. These bets pay 2–1, with the usual house percentage.

Red or Black; Even or Odd; Low or High: Except for 0 and 00, every number on the wheel and table is colored red or black, and, being a number between 1 and 36, is either odd or even, and either in the low (1 through 18) or high (19 through 36) half of the scale. The player sits right next to the boxes that receive these bets. Some players bet on color, others on Odd or Even, others on High or Low, and still others bet on combinations of two or three of these even-money opportunities. Most system players concentrate their attention here, seeking the trends, the continuation or reversal of trends, and/or the combinations of trends that will reward careful study, intense planning, and an upright life. In due course, every possible trend, continuation, reversal, and combination turns up, making some folks lucky and some less so. (See Chapter Two: "Money Management and Betting Systems" for further details.) Each of these bets pays even money—1–1. Vigorish: 5.26 percent.

GUIDING PRINCIPLES

Inasmuch as it is easy for anyone to play Craps with a house percentage of less than 1 percent and Blackjack and Baccarat at comparably small disadvantage, American Roulette is no part of a bargain. Nevertheless, it provides relaxation and atmosphere and, in any case, can bring no harm to anyone who approaches it with open eyes.

As suggested by the uniformity of the 5.26 percent vig on all but one of the many possible bets, one bet is pretty much as good as another. However, regret awaits persons who spread a multitude of chips around the layout before every turn of the wheel, hoping to outnumber the confounded thing and win more often than lose. The larger the number of bets per turn, the more rapidly the house percentage operates. To delay the effects of the house percentage and make the money last longer, it is advisable to make fewer bets per turn. Players interested in attacking systematically will find that the even-money propositions generally are best, not because they win more money but because they win more frequently than do bets at higher odds. This is true not only in Roulette but in other casino games. The next chapter reviews betting systems that seek maximum advantage from even-money betting.

ROULETTE PATTERN SYSTEMS

Ages ago, somebody noticed that the middle column of the Roulette layout contains eight black numbers and only four red ones. This gave rise to a procedure known as the Black System. Innumerable hucksters have sold it through the mails, promising miracles.

Here is the idea: If you bet $1 on the middle column at the usual odds of 2–1, and $2 on Black at the usual even money, you win $4 when one of the eight middle-column black numbers appears. You win $1 when some other black number appears. If one of the four middle-column red numbers turns up, you break even, having won $2 on that column while losing $2 on Black. Eight chances to win $4! Ten chances to win $1! On 18 of the 38 possibilities built into an American wheel, you win! Moreover, on four other chances, you break even, leaving the house with a paltry 16 chances to get back at you! True. *Except* that the house takes $3 from you on each of those 16 occasions, making you a $6 loser on the average 38 turns and maintaining its vigorish at the customary 5.26 percent. As always, the house percentage remains impregnable, and you only lose your money more rapidly.

A variation emphasizes the presence of eight red numbers

in the third column and proceeds with $1 bets on that column and $2 bets on Red. Still another approach favors a $1 bet on that column and another $1 bet on Black. The net loss now becomes only $4 on a typical sequence of 38 turns, and the house percentage stands undisturbed at 5.26. Again there is no advantage, and you are only losing your money faster by placing so many bets at once.

In European Roulette, which uses a 37-number wheel with only one zero, it is possible to delay disaster for hours on end by risking large amounts in cannily proportioned bets on all numbers but one of the 37. We'll come to that and other 37-number wheel miracles—none of which work forever—when we examine the European game.

BIASED WHEELS

If a wheel is the least bit out of balance, or if loosened frets have made one or more of the numbered compartments wider than others, long-term results will demonstrate that something is out of kilter. Money has been made by gamblers studious enough to perceive such conditions and bet accordingly. Anyone willing to spend days tallying the outcome of each turn at a single table is welcome to try. That kind of exercise does not come under the heading of recreational gambling, of course. For want of a more high-flown description, let us call it a waste of time. No doubt wheels do get out of balance once in a rare while. A sophomore dedicated to beating the establishment at its own game might spend two years hunting for a wheel sufficiently out of phase to reward large wagers on whatever numbers are favored by gravity. Having found the wheel—a less than completely inevitable conclusion to so heroic a search—the player would not likely win enough to pay for all the time and effort. The casino management would notice the peculiar betting activity and the more peculiar table losses and would decommission the wheel for overhaul. Such things have happened.

Theories of biased wheels, blended with theories of number patterns, are grist for the casino's mill. With no discouragement from the house, and in some places with its active help, system players carry tally sheets and/or tables that show what numbers are the nearest neighbors of the numbers that have been winning. Having discerned a pattern (which is easy, because everything at every gambling table fits into a pattern of some kind or other), the player bets on it. Chances of winning remain the same as if, unencumbered by printed matter, the same player fooled around on Odd or Even, Red or Black, High or Low. Which is to say that hardly any wheels are biased. And, given an unbiased wheel, the house percentage remains effective no matter how the player bets.

EUROPEAN ROULETTE

The European wheel has only 37 compartments—36 numbers and a 0, but lacking the American 00. This reduces the house percentage to 2.7.

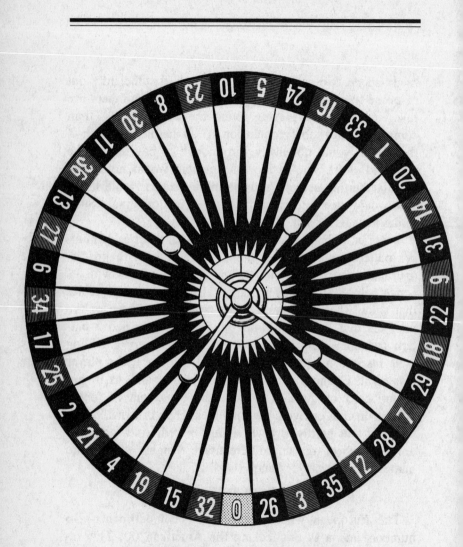

EUROPEAN ROULETTE WHEEL

At Monte Carlo and a few other resorts, the percentage on even-money bets drops to about 1.35, thanks to a feature known as *en prison*. When the 0 comes up, the bettor on Red, Black, High, Low, Even, or Odd neither wins nor loses. Instead, the croupier impounds the bet until a subsequent turn of the wheel determines what is to happen to the chips. Example: You bet on Black. The ball lands in 0. The bet goes to prison. On the next turn, the ball again hits 0. The bet remains in prison. If the next turn produces Red, the house gets your money and players who had bet on Black have their chips returned. But if the number after the 0 had come up Black, you would have had your chips returned and people betting on Red would have lost.

An associated feature is called *partage*. Rather than awaiting disposition of an imprisoned bet by the next turn of the wheel, the player may choose to retrieve half the bet, with the house getting the other half. The vig remains 1.35 percent. Either way, Monte Carlo-style Roulette is a much fairer game than the American brand.

European wheels are found in Nevada, but not with the *en prison* or *partage* opportunities. More than one horrified expert has commented on the phenomenon that finds the unfamiliar European-style table empty while crowds pay through the nose at a 38-slot wheel across the aisle.

Atlantic City's legal casinos modify the customary 5.26 vig on even-money bets by confiscating merely half of the player's money when the ball lands in 0 or 00. This version of *partage* lowers the house percentage to 2.6 on even-money bets, leaving it at the hallowed 5.26 on all others.

EUROPEAN LINGO

European Roulette is played in French. Here is the terminology:

En Plein: A straight bet on a number.
A Cheval: A split bet on two numbers.
Transversale Plein: A three-number street.
Un Carré: A corner bet on four numbers.
Sixaine: A bet on six numbers.
Colonne: A column bet on 12 numbers.
Douzaine: A bet on the first, second, or third 12 numbers.
Rouge et Noir: Red and Black.
Pair et Impair: Even and Odd.
Passe et Manque: High (19 through 36) and Low (1 through 18).
Faites vos jeux: "Make your bets," says the croupier.
Rien ne va plus: "No more bets."

EUROPEAN PATTERN PLAY

With the *en prison* attraction, the one-zero game is comfortably close to an even proposition. Literally thousands of schemes have been devised for the lofty purpose of beating the wheel by catching its probabilities off guard. For one elementary example, if the wheel be turned 1,500 times in 15 series of 100 turns each, the chances are substantial that one's favorite number (anybody for Number 7?) will have turned up at least once in no fewer than 14 of the series. To be sure, the chances of the number appearing on any *particular* turn are only one in 37. But, as usual, there is more to probability than meets the inexperienced, non-mathematical eye. Indeed, the favorite Number 7 (or whatever) is quite likely to appear by the 23d or 24th turn.

Knowing this, plus the good news that any number is odds-on (1–14) to win during a series of 100 spins, a player might wager one chip on the same number for 30 spins. If it fails to win in that time, the bet increases to two chips for 15 more turns. If still no winner, play continues as follows:

Bets 46 through 56: 3 chips.
Bets 57 through 64: 4 chips.
Bets 65 through 72: 5 chips.
Bets 73 through 78: 6 chips.
Bets 79 through 82: 7 chips.
Bets 83 through 86: 8 chips.
Bets 87 through 90: 9 chips.

Assuming that the house limit has not yet been reached, the player bets 10 chips on turns 91 through 94, 11 on 95 through 97, and 12 on 98 through 100. If the number has still not won, the player shrugs gallantly and retreats to the bar. But if, as is considerably more likely to happen on any random occasion, the number comes up in time, the profit ranges between 11 and 52 chips.

The formula appears with a superabundance of others in the optimistically titled and thoroughly fascinating *How To Win at Roulette*, by Norman Squire, which is available for $2.50 from Gambler's Book Club, 630 South 11th Street, Box 4115, Las Vegas, Nevada 89106. A bimonthly publication of the same firm, *Casino & Sports*, presented in its undated Volume 2 an even more likely plan which it called "Roulette Dinner." In this one, the player bets proportioned amounts on an astounding total of 36 numbers in well-founded hope of winning one chip (enough to purchase dinner): A bet of 72 chips goes on *Passe* (High); 8 on numbers 14 and 15, *A Cheval* (Split); 12 on 16, 17, and 18, *Transversale Plein* (Street); 48 on *Premier Douzaine* (1st 12), and 3 on 0, *En Plein* (Straight). The only number uncovered by the total wager of 143 chips is 13. When anything but 13 or 0 turns up, the profit is one chip. If the 0 wins, the player gets 108 chips and the *Passe* chips go into prison. By opting for *partage*, the player gets 36 additional chips for a total of 144 and the intended profit!

Someone who contemplates a European gambling jaunt and would like to spend happy hours at the wheel should obtain the Squire book. Nothing in it modifies the inexorable house percentage, of course. But, like the best of the wagering systems that appear in the next chapter, the best of these Roulette patterns tend to defer loss and increase pleasure.

AMERICAN ROULETTE PLUS

Wheels with 39 numbers, including 0, 00, and 000, are not unheard of and should be boycotted. The house percentage is an exorbitant 7.69. In addition, some places try to pay off column and other dozens bets at "2 *for* 1," which is only even money instead of the customary 2 to 1. Nobody should patronize such a game, even though it might be the only one in town.

SUMMARY

STRATEGY FOR BEGINNERS

Prefer a European wheel to an American. Select a betting procedure from Chapter Two and play it on one of the even-money propositions—Red or Black, High or Low, Even or Odd. Remember that the winning chances of Red always equal those of Black, and the same reality governs the other two even-money alternatives. Therefore, it does not matter at all where you place your chips. You can play Red all night, or alternate Red and High, or alternate Odd and Black and Low, or play any other combination. Select any pattern that pleases. After you become accustomed to the routines of the table and the minor arithmetic of some betting system, you may want to bet on two or three out-comes at once—for example, Red, High, and Even. Bear in mind that this hastens the vacuum-cleaner effect of the house percentage.

STRATEGY FOR VETERANS

If you do not have a favorite pattern of play, use a bet-ing system (see Chapter Two: "Money Management and Betting Systems") on the columns or dozens in any pattern that intrigues you. When you win, you win more quickly. And when you lose, you lose more quickly. This liberates you for serious business at Craps, Blackjack, or Baccarat, where the percentages are better.

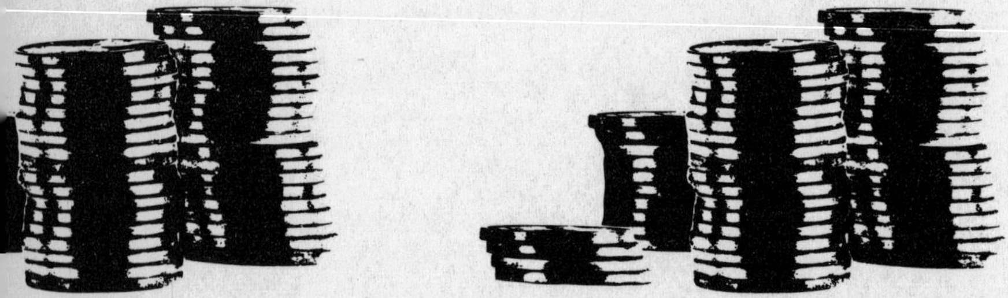

TWO:

MONEY MANAGEMENT AND BETTING SYSTEMS

=====================================

FOR MOST OF US, CASINO GAMBLING IS A SPECIAL TREAT TO which we travel many miles at no small expense. The excursions are most enjoyable when we manage our funds intelligently enough to get what we came for—a full measure of recreation at the tables. A money-management plan works if it (a) strengthens the effort to win and (b) assures the availability of funds for as many table sessions as the player had in mind at the beginning of the trip.

The first prerequisite is willing ability to segregate gambling capital from funds needed for other purposes. You should make this decision *before* entering the casino—and stick to it. If I seem to be advising you not to gamble with the meal money, no offense is intended. I also advise that gambling money not be wasted on food or rent.

Having set aside a gambling bankroll, you should divide it into portions—an equal amount for each contemplated fling at the tables. Good money managers do that in advance and refuse to tinker with the arrangement in the heat of play. They always have more fun than, for example, the plunger who blows the whole bundle on the first afternoon and spends the next two days moping beneath a poolside umbrella.

Interestingly, and altogether in keeping with the *Catch-22* nature of casino gambling, the kind of money management that sustains play for the full term of one's visit rarely produces huge winnings. The player most likely to go home with a doubled bankroll is the one who disdains the prudence advocated in these pages. That player bets the entire wallet on the first Craps roll or Baccarat hand of the very first session, doubling the money if the bet wins and walking to the bus terminal if it loses. Mathematics demonstrates that the chances of doubling one's betting capital diminish as the number of bets increases. And the chances of ruin—complete loss of capital—become higher. In other words, if you stay there long enough, the casino wipes you out.

No sensible person need remain that long. I have never been able to understand why otherwise useful gambling treatises always emphasize extreme alternatives, as if no middle ground existed between doubling one's money and going broke. In the Introduction, I deplored gambling fever and mentioned the principle of limiting both loss and gain at each table session. When implemented with a sensible betting system, this principle almost eliminates the possibility of losing the entire betting fund but does not eliminate the possibility of substantial profit. Indeed, gamblers who take this approach can expect to defray the cost of an occasional vacation. And when results fall short of that, the gamblers at least have the satisfaction of playing the planned number of times during the allotted days and nights, and losing no more than they can afford.

THE GRAND STRATEGY

You have arrived for a two-day stay, prepared to lose $400 but determined to win if you can. You want to play twice a day—four sessions in all. You therefore are planning to lose no more than $100 per session. If you are also prepared to quit a session after winning $50, you have a fighting chance of reaching the objective every time, and a quite good chance of doing it three times. If you can settle for less than $50 in winnings at an individual session, chances of success improve still more.

Far from prescribing an amount to be risked, I am simply trying to propound a principle. Whether you are willing to lose $400 or $4,000, the chances of finishing ahead improve when the gain at each session is limited to an amount considerably smaller than the sum that you are willing to lose. Obviously, if you are willing to lose $1,000 but are prepared to quit the table after winning only $200, you would have brighter prospects than if you hung on hoping to nudge your gain up to $400 or $500. This strategy does not overcome the house percentage. Nothing can do that.

But it steers a pleasurable course between the ridiculous alternatives of double-the-capital and ruin. Limiting both loss and gain, confining activity to the least unfavorable bets in the least unfavorable games, and parceling out funds in conformity with a decent betting system, the player remains safe from harm.

GAMBLING SYSTEMS IN GENERAL

Now that computer studies of gambling probability are available in any bookstore and the word has spread, few adults seriously believe that a betting system can undo the house percentage. Casino games are designed to place the customer at a disadvantage in any long-term series of transactions. Accordingly, a betting system can do no more than enable you to exploit the temporary advantages that arise, while avoiding grave penalty when advantage is absent.

An ideal system would enable the player to risk more chips on winning bets than on losing ones. The ideal is beyond sure reach, but some procedures increase the likelihood sufficiently to yield a profit even when losing bets outnumber winning ones—provided that the wins and losses occur in patterned sequences favorable to the particular system.

Some of the most popular systems assure a relatively high probability of numerous small gains, all of which go down the pipes when fate supplies the inevitable (if considerably less likely) big loss. Other systems reverse these probabilities, subjecting the player to highly likely small losses, with a remote chance of large gain.

Whatever the system, it eventually fails anyone who plays too doggedly, risking ruin in a doomed effort to break the bank. Thus, a player's willingness to limit both losses and gains becomes paramount. Several systems are comfortably compatible with that approach. We begin with one that is not.

THE MARTINGALE

We glanced off this one on an earlier page. Known to some as the Double-Up Progression, it is one of the oldest, most widely used, and least satisfactory ways to gamble. Based on the fallacy that some "law of averages" decrees frequent trend reversals and a kind of equilibrium between Red and Black (in Roulette), Pass and Don't Pass (in Craps), and other ventures that pay even money to the winning bettor, the Martingale requires the player to double the bet after each loss. If Roulette or Craps were actually even games, like coin tossing, the Martingale would be more useful than it is, but would still leave much to be desired. The fact is that someone who falls behind in a game of Heads and Tails is more likely to lose than to win. Regardless of how long play may continue, it is unlikely that someone who trails by, say, eleven unfavorable flips of a coin, will ever catch up. Roulette compounds the disadvantage. The chances of Red winning are smaller than the chances that a coin will come up Heads—because of the 0 or 00 on the wheel. And even when Red wins, the house does not pay the winning bettor enough to defray the cost of the losing bets.

So where does this leave the Martingale player? For one thing, the system produces many small wins and relatively few large losses. Yet, the losses are both inevitable and devastating. For example, the house limit prevents a player from continuing to double bets forever, until a winning turn finally occurs. In most places, someone who has lost eight or nine successive Martingale bets is not allowed to double again, having reached the limit. At a table that accepts $1 bets but imposes an upper limit of $500, the doubler reaches that limit after nine consecutive losses, during which $511 have departed the bankroll. Here is the betting sequence:

$1, $2, $4, $8, $16, $32, $64, $128, $256—for a total of $511.

If the table has a $1,000 limit, the player may try a tenth bet of $512 in the gallant effort to win a grand total of $1. That statement is correct. The size of each Martingale bet is sufficient only to yield the same profit that would have been made if the first bet in the series had won.

Naturally, many Martingale players gravitate to casinos that permit as many as 10 successive double-ups. In downtown Las Vegas it is possible to find tables that accept wagers as low as 25 cents, with a top limit of $250. Beginning at 25 cents, the series reaches $128 on the tenth attempt, by which time $127.75 have been expended in hope of winning a quarter. If the tenth bet loses, the player is down $255.75 and can double no more.

An imaginary gambler who played that kind of 25-cent progression the clock around for 100 years would win more than 99 percent of all the sequences, pocketing many quarters. During that hypothetical century, the player would also lose millions of times, because of the house limit. The net loss would correspond almost exactly with the house percentage. At American Roulette, for example, the loss would be just about 5.26 percent of all the billions wagered.

In real life, not many gamblers are consciously willing to risk $255.75 to make 25 cents on a dice roll that gives them a somewhat less than even chance of winning the 25 cents. At the beginning of each series, the chances of winning the quarter are above 99 percent, to be sure, but the laws of probability work in wondrous ways. If the chances of loss are, let us say, fewer than 5 in 1,000 plays, one of those rare losses can crop up at any time, including one's first evening in the casino.

Variations: In quest of larger profits, some gamblers use a steeper Martingale progression, adding a fixed sum to each doubled bet. For example, instead of progressing in the familiar sequence of $1, $2, $4, the bettor might add an extra dollar each time, making the progression $1, $3, $7. This is called the Great Martingale. When successful, it produces the higher profits, as desired, but it encounters the house limit more rapidly and, therefore, more often.

THE ANTI-MARTINGALE

Instead of doubling the bet after each loss, this goes in the opposite direction, doubling after each *win* and dropping back to the minimum one-unit bet after a loss. Carried to extremes, it offers an infinitesimal chance of huge profits. Meanwhile, it reaps many small losses and must lead in due time to a completely vacant billfold. But the guiding principle has real virtue, especially when implemented by a player who has no intention of going to extremes.

Instead of doubling up after every win in the small hope of hitting the nine wins in succession that will bring one abaft of the table limit, a sensible player can limit the number of parlays (known in Roulette circles as *parolis*) and draw down the original stake after the *second* successive win. For example, if betting on Pass at Craps, the first bet might be $1. If it wins, the player has $2, and lets it ride. If the outcome is favorable, the player has $4 and can withdraw the original $1, continuing play for one more roll, but with the casino's $3.

Endless variations are possible. Instead of pocketing the original dollar, the player might choose to take $2, making

66

the third bet only $2. If that one wins, the stake is back to $4 again, at which point the player might withdraw nothing, or $1 or $2, depending on mood or plan or both. Play of this kind is a far cry from the original Anti-Martingale, the purpose of which was to get rich on an occurrence that seldom materializes—eight or nine successive wins. Assuming that the first bet in the series was $1, the player would end a successful eight-bet progression with $256, including the original dollar. The house limit would prevent further doubling up. Note that the actual odds against a winning streak of eight Reds or Blacks or Evens or Odds are about 390–1. Persons who accept 255–1 on 390–1 shots are very popular with casino managements and do not win consistently at Roulette or any other game.

A stringently modified Anti-Martingale is among the better ways to tackle the even-money challenges of Craps or Baccarat or even Roulette. Its advantages over the Martingale are considerable. It allows the player to win quickly, without having to risk hundreds of dollars trying to recoup early losses. It also allows a winning player to operate with the house's money. And when it loses, it costs only one betting unit per loss.

A simple paroli of two or three bets is also superior to flat betting, in which the player risks the same amount each time. To illustrate the difference, I shall now list the possibilities that arise in any two-bet series. "W" stands for win and "L" for lose.

	FIRST BET	SECOND BET
A.	W	L
B.	W	W
C.	L	L
D.	L	W

Those are the only possible outcomes of a two-bet series. The flat bettor will risk one unit at a time. The two-bet paroli bettor begins with a bet of one unit, and lets the proceeds ride for one more bet if the first bet wins. If the first bet loses, the next is a one-unit bet to begin another two-bet parlay attempt.

In Sequence A, the flat bettor breaks even, winning one and losing one. The adherent of the Anti-Martingale ends with a net loss of one, having let the money from the winning first bet ride on the losing second bet. In Sequence B, the flat bettor wins two units, but the other gambler's paroli wins, yielding a profit of three units. In Sequence C, both players drop two units. In Sequence D, the straight bettor again breaks even, but the paroli bettor ends at an advantage. The first bet loses a unit, but the second becomes the first attempt at a new paroli. It wins, giving our friend a free shot at a third bet on which a win will produce a profit of three and a loss will cost only one unit. Note that the two-bet paroli fancier can expect to encounter this pleasant situation about 25 percent of the time.

Temptation is strong to try four- and five-bet parolis, but

should be resisted. I believe that an Anti-Martingale with a two-bet paroli is a decent way to battle the even-money propositions, especially when the dice, cards, or wheel are not too adverse. I particularly like the two-bet paroli as an entertainment with which to conclude a session in which winnings have been achieved by means of some other system. Instead of quitting the table immediately after reaching the pledged stop-gain limit, it is fun to retrieve one of the casino's chips from the jacket pocket and try a two-bet paroli or two. Then leave smiling.

THE D'ALEMBERT

You may have heard of this as the Pyramid, the Up-and-Down, or the Seesaw. Its principle is to increase the bet by one unit after each loss and to decrease the bet by one unit after each win. As anyone will realize in a moment's reflection, this means that when winning bets are as numerous as losing ones, the gambler should have one unit of profit for each winning bet. Each series begins with a bet of one unit and terminates if that first wager wins. Otherwise, the next bet is two units, and the series proceeds up and down until, one hopes, a new one-unit bet presents itself, meaning that the series has ended and profits are in hand.

Some examples of D'Alembert series:

69

UNITS BET	RESULT	BANKROLL
1	Lose 1	−1
2	Lose 2	−3
3	Win 3	Even
2	Win 2	+2
1	Win 1	+3
1	Win 1	+4
1	Lose 1	+3
2	Lose 2	+1
3	Lose 3	−2
4	Lose 4	−6
5	Win 5	−1
4	Win 4	+3

The bettor has lost as often as won, yet finishes ahead by three units. When wins and losses occur at the same rate in a different yet equally likely sequence, the net result is less cheering:

UNITS BET	RESULT	BANKROLL
1	Win 1	+1
1	Win 1	+2
1	Win 1	+3
1	Win 1	+4
1	Lose 1	+3
2	Lose 2	+1
3	Lose 3	−2
4	Lose 4	−6
5	Win 5	−1
4	Lose 4	−5
5	Lose 5	−10
6	Win 6	−4

Like the Martingale, the D'Alembert succeeds when the dice or wheel or cards provide patterns of short losing streaks followed by winning streaks. It also holds its own during periods of "choppy" play unmarked by lengthy streaks of wins or losses. But it fails utterly when consecutive wins occur at the beginning of play and are followed by a prolonged succession of losses. The D'Alembert or Martingale player who falls substantially behind is quite unlikely to catch up. If sufficiently stubborn, such a player has a large chance of encountering the house limit. The reader who wants to take a chance on D'Alembert play should do so only if determined to impose a severe limit on personal losses per session, leaving the table long before approaching the house limit.

Variations: Some prefer to increase by two units after each loss, which works when it works and hastens difficulties when it does not. Others believe in starting each series at a level higher than one—perhaps as high as five or ten units, and increasing or decreasing by one after each respective loss or win. Again, profits increase but so do losses.

THE CONTRA-D'ALEMBERT

This time the player *increases* the bet by one unit after each win, reducing it by one after each loss. The effect is

71

much like the play of an Anti-Martingale, in which a winner chooses to withdraw all but one unit of profit on each successive winning bet of the series after the second. When consecutive losses occur, the bet reduces itself to one unit, there to remain until things improve. A two-bet Anti-Martingale paroli is preferable, dropping to one unit immediately after each loss and supplying a profit of three units after each sequence of two wins. The Contra-D'Alembert loses as much as the other during unsuccessful streaks and wins too slowly during successful ones.

THE LABOUCHÈRE

Known to some as Cancellation or Labby, this is less abrupt than the Martingale and lends itself to variations in which, if lengthy losing streaks do not occur, profits may accrue even when losing plays outnumber winning ones. Unless the gambler is a mental marvel, paper and pencil are needed.

For a sample, write three numbers in a row: 1, 2, 3. The first bet is the sum of the outside numbers—1 + 3 = 4. Your first bet is $4. If it wins, cross out the outside numbers: 1, 2, 3. The next bet is $2. But if the first bet loses, write the loss at the end of the line: 1, 2, 3, 4. The next bet, like all other Labby bets, is the sum of the outside numbers In this case, $5. If it wins, cross out the 1 and the 4, leaving

72

the 2 and 3, which are added to make the next bet, which is again $5. And so on.

A winning series throws off profits equal to the sum of the original numbers, multiplied by the number of dollars per betting unit. Variations are endless. Some begin with four or five numbers. These need not follow the usual 1, 2, 3 sequence but might be 1, 1, 1, 1. Or 1, 2, 5.

The larger the original numbers on the list, the larger the bets become after successive losses, and the closer the player approaches (a) the house limit or (b) the self-imposed limit on losses for the particular session. As often as not, however, the player with a moderate profit objective will achieve it when using the system at Baccarat. Needless to say, loss stalks a persistent Labby player who neglects to quit when moderately ahead and allows bets to approach house limits. In the end, the net loss is almost exactly the total amount bet at all sessions, multiplied by the house percentage on the game that was played.

Apart from that inescapable reality, and the nuisance of paper and pencil, the chief disadvantage of cancellation is that the player lacks control over the maximum bet. Someone playing an Anti-Martingale with a two-bet paroli knows for certain that the maximum bet will be two units and the maximum loss on such a bet will be one unit—the amount staked on the first bet of each two-bet series. But when the cancellation method hits a losing streak, one is obliged to keep punting until stopped by the house limit or a personal stop-loss limit. I suppose that someone with a loss limit of 40 units could resolve in advance to terminate any cancellation series when its deficit reached a total of 20 units. The player could then begin a fresh series. But I doubt if many readers would enjoy the paperwork.

OSCAR'S GRIND

This is my favorite. Properly managed, it wins many more table sessions than it loses. It often wins even when losing bets outnumber winning ones. It works most satisfactorily when the betting unit is not more than 2 or 3 percent of the sum that the player is prepared to lose at the particular table session. Thus, a $5 betting unit should be backed by a readily available fund of not less than $250. As usual, the player should be content to discontinue the session when winnings are half or less of the allotted capital. The $5 betting unit would call for a stop-gain limit of $100 or $125.

The celebrated gambling mathematician, Dr. Allan N. Wilson, introduced the system in his immensely informative book, *The Casino Gambler's Guide* (see additional details in Appendix A). Wilson reported that Julian Braun, the foremost computer analyst of gambling probabilities, had found that a player who used the system on even-money Craps wagers with a betting unit of $1 would risk reaching a $500 house limit no more often than once in 4,250 sessions. It stands to reason that someone whose own loss limit is considerably short of the house's maximum bet would be quite secure. And that is how this system seems to work out in real life. When making $10 bets with a stop-loss of $400 and quitting when $200 ahead, I have paid—thanks to Oscar—for more than one trip to Caribbean and Nevada casinos. I win about three sessions in every four.

The originator of the system, a weekend Craps shooter undescribed except as Oscar, told Wilson that he had never left Las Vegas as anything but a winner. The probability was enormous that he would lose someday and that the average loss (as Julian Braun found) would be upward of $13,000 when bucking a $500 house limit. But, as I keep saying, no reason exists to play that way. The personal stop-loss and stop-gain are powerful allies.

Enough of this suspense. The system probably is an off-shoot of the D'Alembert. The goal of each series of bets is a profit of one betting unit. When that profit is in hand, the player pockets the chip and begins a new series. When the number of pocketed chips equals the prescribed limit on gain, the player cashes in and takes a recess.

The first bet in each series is one unit. If it loses, the next bet is also one unit and the player notes that a loss will now bring the deficit of the series to two units. After a loss, the next bet is always the same size as the bet just lost. When a series is losing, proceeds of a successful bet are not pocketed but the next bet is increased by one unit. No bet ever is larger than may be necessary to end a series with a profit of one unit.

To illustrate, the player loses the first five bets in a series, and is now five units behind. The next bet of one unit wins, leaving the series four down. The bet after that is two units (pursuing the principle of increasing the bet by one unit after a win). If that bet loses, the series is down by six. The next bet is two (the principle of not modifying the bet after a loss). If that bet wins, the series is down four and the next bet is three (the formula increase of one unit). If that bet wins, the series is now down one unit and the next bet is not increased. As stated earlier, no bet is ever large enough to net a series profit of more than one unit. In this example, the next bet is two—to convert a loss of one into a net gain of one. If it loses, the series is now down three and the bet remains two. If that wins, the series is back to one down and the formula requires a bet of two to put everything into the black by one. The profit goes into the pocket and a new series begins with a bet of one unit.

When things go well at Craps, Baccarat, or Blackjack, this system may win its per-session quota in a very few minutes, depositing the player at a crossroads. You did not travel all the way to the casino to quit after a quarter of an hour. On the other hand, you are sworn to quit when moderately ahead. To resolve the dilemma and strengthen the all-important sense of mastery, get up from the table and take a walk or a drink. Resume play later, preferably with a new loss limit no higher than the amount you have just won. If you lose it, you have simply handed the casino's money back, but have squandered none of your own.

Sometimes losing bets and winning ones come in short

clusters that pretty much balance each other. Again, Oscar can be counted on to win, but it will take longer. And, of course, occasions arise when Oscar plunges deep into the red. As the researches of Julian Braun demonstrated, the procedure almost always can bail itself out. But I believe that this takes too long, risks too much, and, in any case, is likely to bring the conservative player to the stop-loss limit. Once again, temptation arises. If the system is so dependable, and the probability of ruin so slight, why not press on? One answer is that recreational gamblers are not at their sharpest when fatigued. Neither do they enjoy themselves in that condition. For that reason, I think it a mistake to let an Oscar series even approach the per-session stop-loss limit. Instead, I prefer to terminate any series as soon as (a) it is more than 10 units down and (b) a loss on the next bet would leave it 20 units down. Interestingly enough, this state of affairs may be reached when one has already pocketed 20 or more winning chips. To terminate the poor series and either take a walk or start an entirely new series is extremely advantageous. If the pattern of table play changes, as it does so frequently, one may soon find the profit pocket bulging and the gain limit at hand.

SUMMARY

STRATEGY FOR BEGINNERS

Use the tables in Appendix B for dry-run Oscar play at Baccarat and the even-money wagers of Craps and Roulette.

Become familiar with the easy counting procedures. At the casino, play the system on the same simple wagers. Having reached the stop-gain limit, take one of the casino's chips from your profit pocket and play a two-bet paroli. If it wins, play another. If that wins, play still another and then stop play for the session, in a well-deserved spirit of self-esteem. And if you lose, quit at the stop-loss limit and congratulate yourself. You have budgeted wisely and will have ample funds for other sessions throughout your stay in the resort.

STRATEGY FOR VETERANS

As you undoubtedly know, the best way to gamble is with the casino's money, if you can only manage to get some of it. That being the case, consider the possibility of using rigorous stop-loss and stop-gain limits during the earlier sessions of your casino vacation. Using Oscar's Grind, give these first periods of play every opportunity to build a fund of the house's money for more aggressive gambling in the later sessions. You then will be able to attack with an Anti-Martingale of two or three bets per series, preferably withdrawing the amount of the initial wager after the second bet in each three-bet paroli. You cannot lose much that way, but can win a lot, especially if your confine your bets to the least disadvantageous ones offered in whatever game you enjoy the most.

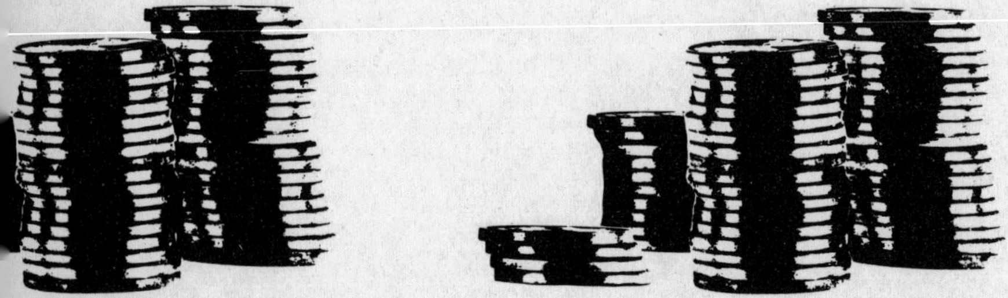

THREE:
CRAPS

AT A WELL-RUN CRAPS TABLE, THE DICE ROLL AS OFTEN as 200 times an hour. This is the fastest of casino games. It also is the noisiest and, on early acquaintance, the most confusing. Piles of chips whisk from place to place in mysterious patterns. A personage called the "stickman" brandishes a long-handled implement while spieling like a midway barker. Some of the players growl a lot. Others emit wild cries. Most bet with tense purposefulness, as if they knew exactly what they were doing. The apprehensive newcomer tends to steer clear.

Fuss and feathers. Nothing to be intimidated by. Despite the air of expertise, the veteran Craps enthusiast is usually a dedicated patsy. If the ignorance that prevails among Craps players were not so appalling, it would be funny. Craps is an idiotically simple game. In a few minutes, any beginner can learn all that is worth knowing. In a few minutes, take my word, the novice becomes a reigning expert.

The virtue of Craps is that it is mighty entertaining and

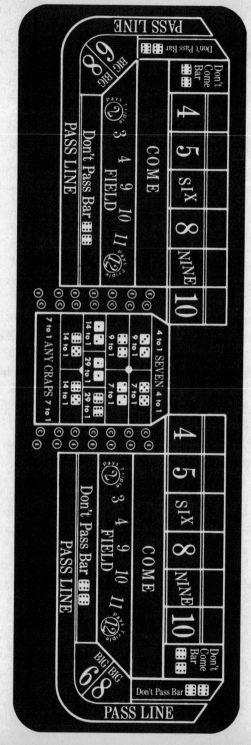

CRAPS LAYOUT

comparatively fair to the competent player. It provides a splendid run for your money. Example: In some U.S. casinos, a knowing gambler can play Craps against a house percentage about one-ninth of the vigorish exacted at American Roulette. This is the best deal obtainable at any casino table, unless you care to include the brand of Blackjack played by a few dozen sharpers who make a career of it.

Craps is too good to be left to those who play it most. After mastering the few bits of information needed for sensible betting, the reader absolutely must have a go at the table. No basis exists for self-consciousness. Nothing you do has the slightest effect on the game or on the luck of the other players. They are not even your opponents. They play not against you and each other but against the house. If they knew how to play, they would beat the house once in a while. You'll see.

THE LAYOUT

A Craps table is about as long and wide as a regulation billiards table but has high sides to keep the two dice in bounds. The inner walls at each end are cushioned, so that thrown dice will bounce energetically and land at random. The pattern of betting possibilities printed on the table surface varies with local or regional policy but never includes all possible bets. It generally resembles the layout in our illustration.

The players cluster on either side of the stickman, from one end of the table to the other, but not intruding on the opposite long side, which is the preserve of the boxman and dealers. With frequent assistance from a dealer, players put their chips in whatever spaces represent the bets they want to make.

THE TABLE CREW

The presiding authority is the *boxman*, whose title derives from the responsibility of selling chips and depositing the money in a slot that feeds the cash box. Seated at a point of vantage across the table from the stickman, and flanked by standing dealers, the boxman oversees the transactions between dealers and players. He tries to make sure that the dealers follow the customer's instructions, placing chips in the desired areas of the layout beyond the player's reach, and, of course, make accurate payoffs.

When a player-dealer disagreement arises over the amount that the player thought had been won or lost on a roll, or if they dispute the nature of the bet that the player had intended, the boxman resolves the issue. An argumentative player usually gets the benefit of the doubt on first complaint. Unless clearly justified in a subsequent protest, such a player is likely to be ushered out of the establishment on order of the boxman's superior, the pit boss.

Beyond helping the players to bet and paying off winners,

dealers are responsible for placement of a puck (often called a "buck") in the numbered area that indicates the shooter's point (defined below). Meanwhile, across the table, the _stickman_ uses a long, bent wand to push the dice to the player whose turn it is to roll the dice. He also announces the outcome of each roll, advises the player when to roll, tries to keep the action going at a pace comfortable for the customers, and persistently solicits bets on the most alluringly high-odds propositions, which happen invariably to be the bets most advantageous to the house.

THE PROCEDURE

When the table opens for business and the gamblers have begun to materialize at its perimeter, the stickman pushes the dice to the player at his extreme right. That person is the _shooter_—the one who rolls the dice. The rules permit any player to decline the privilege. In such circumstances, or when the rules (as we shall see) require the shooter to relinquish the dice, the role of shooter rotates clockwise—from right to left on the player's side of the table. Anyone who can find room at the table can play. And anyone, whether acting as shooter or not, can bet on or against a successful roll of the dice. That is, the shooter is permitted to bet against the shooter if so minded. And other players may bet on the shooter and often do.

The shooter is obliged to cast the dice so that they

bounce off the inner wall at the other end of the table. To facilitate this all-important bounce and rotation of the dice, some places require the shooter to toss the cubes over an intervening string stretched parallel to the object wall.

TERMINOLOGY

To make sense of Craps, merely reading about it or attempting real play at a casino table, it is essential to understand the basic jargon.

A successful roll or series of rolls is called a *Pass*. Players who wish to bet that the shooter will be successful can place bets on *Pass*. Those who want to bet that the shooter will be unsuccessful can bet on *Don't Pass*.

The shooter's first roll *per sequence* is known as the *come out*. If the dice turn up a 7 or 11—a *natural*—all who bet on Pass win the bets at once and the shooter winds up for a new come out.

When the come-out roll yields a 4, 5, 6, 8, 9, or 10, that number becomes the shooter's *point*. The shooter now wins (passes) if the point repeats on a subsequent roll before a 7 appears. After making a point, the shooter rolls a new come out. If the 7 turns up after the come out but before the point appears, the player has *sevened out*, meaning that Pass bets lose, Don't Pass bets win, and the shooter loses the dice to the adjoining player, clockwise.

When the come out is a 2, 3, or 12—a *crap*—all who

have bet on Pass lose their chips, but the shooter is allowed to retain the dice for a new come out. Crap also wins for *some* Don't Pass bettors, as explained later.

Bets may be made before every throw of the dice, and always are, but not by gamblers interested in minimizing the house percentage, which varies according to the nature of the bet. We shall get to that. But, first, let us see the simple pattern of 36 dice combinations which underlie the probabilities of the game, determine who gets what at the table, and, in combination with the house odds, give the casino its percentage of the wagered money.

THE DICE AND THE ODDS

A die is a cube. Each side bears a different number of identifying dots, from one to six. A pair of rolled dice can produce any of 36 combinations. The sum of the dots on the upward-facing surfaces of the two dice ranges from a low of 2 to a high of 12. The illustration displays all the possibilities.

Inasmuch as a 7 can be rolled in six different combinations, it can be seen that 7 represents $\frac{6}{36}$ of the possibilities. Therefore, the probability that a 7 will appear is 1 in 6, which can be expressed by the fraction $\frac{1}{6}$. To pursue this kind of thing a bit further, if a 7 can be rolled six ways and a 4 can be rolled only three ways, it becomes clear that a shooter whose point is 4 is more likely than not to seven

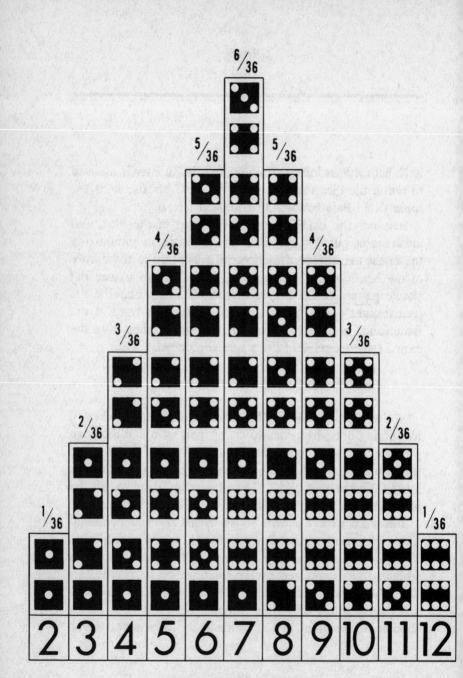

DICE COMBINATIONS

out. The chances are six ways to shoot 7 vs. three ways to shoot 4. That is the same as 2–1. Similarly, someone whose point is 5 has four ways to throw it and is at a disadvantage because of the six ways in which 7 may appear. Now the odds are 6–4 or 3–2.

By the same reasoning, one of the less likely happenings on a come-out roll is a craps (2, 3, or 12), which can be produced in only four ways, whereas a natural 7 or 11 comes eight ways, and a point of 4, 5, 6, 8, 9, or 10 can be established in 24 ways. The odds against craps on the come out therefore are 32–4, which is 8–1. Needless to say, the house pays less than that to a player who bets that 2, 3, or 12 will appear in the next toss.

THE BEST BETS

PASS

The Terms:　A player who bets that the shooter will win is called a *right* or *front-line* bettor and collects from the house when the shooter either rolls a natural 7 or 11 on the come out or repeats a point of 4, 5, 6, 8, 9, or 10 before rolling a 7. The house then pays 1–1, the Pass bettor winning as much money as was risked. The bet loses when the come-out roll is a craps (2, 3, or 12), or if the shooter, having rolled a point on the come out, sevens out before the point reappears.

The Percentage: The house edge on Pass bets is 1.41
percent. What with quick naturals or come-out craps or
lengthier turns (*long hands*)—in which the dice roll many
times before producing the winning point or losing 7—the
average decision at a Craps table takes about three throws.
In an hour of play, wagering $1 on Pass, a player can expect
to encounter about 65 decisions and lose about $1. Obvi-
ously, the loss must greatly exceed that amount on some
occasions, just as the player must finish ahead on others.
But the vig is low, and the Pass bet lends itself to some of
the more entertaining and productive betting systems.

When to Bet: The bet can be made at any time, but
is worthwhile only when placed before the come-out roll,
when 7 and 11 are on the shooter's side. After the come
out, a Pass bet is silly, because the 7 has now become
dangerous.

Where to Bet: Pass bettors are called front-line bettors
because they place their chips in the large area that usually
is closest to their side of the table. Often labeled "Pass" or
"Pass Line," the space may sometimes identify itself merely
as "Line" or "Win."

PASS PLUS FREE ODDS

The Terms: A player with a bet on the Pass Line
usually is allowed to supplement it with a bet at true odds

after the shooter rolls a come-out point. This is a most unusual offer from a casino, and casinos that make the offer do not emphasize it. I have never seen a Craps layout with a clearly labeled space for bets at free odds. Nevertheless, the bet can be made in many places. Mind you, someone who bets at free odds and wins is paid exactly what the point is worth—the house gets absolutely no percentage from this supplementary bet. Here are the proper odds:

POINT	HOUSE PAYS
4 or 10	2–1
5 or 9	3–2
6 or 8	6–5

The Percentage: This is a great bet. It reduces the house vig on Pass betting to .85 percent—85 cents per $100! Furthermore, where competition is brisk among casinos, some may actually offer free *double* odds, allowing a Pass bettor to wager twice as much at free odds as was bet on Pass itself. This reduces the vig to .61 percent.

Important Note: In some places that accept bets at free odds, it is necessary to bet $10 (or some multiple thereof) on Pass. Not being crazy about this kind of action to begin with, the casinos often refuse to pay exact odds of 3–2 to someone who has bet $5 on Pass and then bets another $5 on free odds when the shooter's point is 5 or 9. Other places are more indulgent, allowing the $5 Pass bettor to bet $6 at free odds on 5 or 9. Where double free odds are available, the $5 Pass bettor merely bets $10 at the odds. The nearest dealer will tell you about the current rules of the particular house and will help with the arithmetic, if needed. But you must memorize the odds for yourself.

When to Bet: The free-odds bet can be made or removed after the point is established but before a decision has been reached with a 7 or the point itself. Removal is a mistake, percentages being much more dependable than hunches, and a bet at free odds improving the percentages.

Where to Bet: You have made sure that the place offers single or double free odds. You have memorized the correct odds and have learned from the dealer whether you must risk $10 or a multiple on Pass to qualify for the full benefits. If all systems are go, you place the proper number of chips between yourself and your original Pass bet. The new chips do not go into the Pass Line area itself, but outside it, toward you.

DON'T PASS

The Terms: A player is known as a *wrong* or *back-line* bettor when wagering that the shooter will lose. The house pays such a player 1–1 when the shooter obliges. The terms of the bet are, with one exception, the exact opposite of a Pass bet. The exception is that the house does not pay off on all three come-out craps, usually regarding either the 2 or the 12 as a standoff (or *push* or *tie*). If the legend printed on the back-line betting area announces that the 2 is barred, the bettor's stake is unaffected when the shooter rolls a 2 on the come out. The wagered chips simply remain in place, awaiting a decision on subsequent rolls. Some places bar the 2, others the 12, and still others inflate the vig by barring the 3.

The Percentage:　The house edge on Don't Pass is 1.4 percent, virtually identical with its percentage on Pass. This bite becomes 4.39 percent in resorts that permit the casinos to bar the 3 on the come-out roll. In such places, Don't Pass is a bet to avoid.

When to Bet:　The bet is accepted only before a come-out roll, but the bettor is free to withdraw the chips at any time after a point has been established but before a decision has been reached. Naturally, it is a mistake to withdraw when the shooter is trying to roll a point and the probabilities greatly favor Don't Pass.

Where to Bet:　The chips go on the so-called back line, which usually says "Don't" or "Don't Pass" plus the word "Bar" and a picture of two dice showing a 2 or 12.

DON'T PASS PLUS LAYING THE ODDS

After the come out establishes a shooter's point, some casinos allow Don't Pass bettors to enlarge the action by giving odds that the shooter will crap out before repeating the point. Just as a Pass bettor can obtain the true odds in this situation, the Don't Pass bettor must give them:

POINT	ODDS
4 or 10	2–1
5 or 9	3–2
6 or 8	6–5

Among casinos that offer this opportunity, the terms differ. Some require that the process begin with a Don't Pass bet of $30 (or a multiple thereof). Others allow a larger bet at free odds than on Don't Pass, but only large enough to produce winnings equal to the Don't Pass bet. Still others permit the bettor to double the Don't Pass bet— the back-line equivalent of double free odds on a Pass bet. This can involve a betting risk of as much as $90, but reduces the house advantage to .0459 percent—remarkable for a casino. Where the bettor is permitted to lay only single odds, the house percentage ranges between .69 and .83, depending on the casino's formula.

Even in casinos that accept such action, the bet is seldom seen. The dealer may be unfamiliar with it, needing to consult the boxman or pit boss on whether to allow the bet and how to accommodate it. Players who want to make the bet should discuss it with a floor man before beginning play. Chances are that the bet will be made by handing the required number of chips to a dealer and saying "Odds." The dealer then tilts the chips on the side of the chips that were placed in the back-line area as the player's original Don't bet.

Although the percentage on the combined Don't Pass and Free Odds action is as close to an even proposition as can be found, it ties up (and can liquidate) a good deal of capital. Players with low stop-loss and stop-gain limits usually are more comfortable and get a longer run for their money by playing Pass and taking the odds.

COME

After the shooter produces a point (rather than a crap or a natural) on the come out, anyone at the table can start a game-within-a-game by betting Come. The terms are identical with those of Pass, except that the shooter's next roll is treated as if it were a come out. If the shooter craps out with a 7 on that roll, the Come bet wins as if the 7 were a natural. If the shooter tosses an 11, the Come bet also wins. If the shooter rolls a 2, 3, or 12, the Come bettor loses. If the shooter produces a point, it becomes the Come bettor's point: The dealer moves the bettor's chips from the Come section of the layout to the appropriately numbered box above that section. There they await decision—the appearance of a 7 or a repeat of the particular point. Note that if the shooter rolls his or her *own* point on the first toss after a Come bet is placed, the Come bettor does not win. That point merely becomes the Come bettor's point.

The house percentage on Come is identical with its percentage on Pass. Once made, the bet may not be withdrawn. In most places, furthermore, the player who wins a Come bet must ask for the chips or the dealers assume that the whole pile now is riding on a new come out.

Casinos that offer free odds on Pass usually do the same on Come. This feature, plus the opportunity to place additional Come bets on virtually each roll of the dice, make this area of the layout a favorite location for lovers of fast action. When repeated rolls render no decision for the shooter, the Come bettor is in paradise, profiting from occasional 11's, or the recurrence of 4, 5, 6, 8, 9, or 10, and losing only a little when the first roll after a new Come bet is a 2, 3, or 12. Naturally, when a 7 finally appears, it wipes out all the Come bets that have been sitting in the numbered boxes.

Hedging: After the shooter rolls a point on the come out, Come is a slight hedge for a front-line bettor. Should the next roll be a 7, the win on Come offsets the loss on Pass. Or if the roll is an 11, Come wins but Pass is unaffected. Should the roll produce a 2, 3, or 12, the Come loses, but Pass remains alive. And, of course, if the roll turns up a line point, the Pass-Come bettor now has two points going.

Odds On and Odds Off: To take free odds on Come, hand the required number of chips to the dealer and say, "Odds." The dealer usually balances those chips atop the original Come bet, but slightly off center. When a shooter wins by throwing a point other than one on which the Come bettor has taken free odds, the next roll is, of course, a new come out for the shooter. Many Come bettors dislike that situation, and instruct the dealer, "Odds off on come out" on their own point bets. Or, if they prefer to continue riding with the odds (which is a perfectly good idea), they say, "Odds working."

Too Much Is Too Much: Although the house percentage is low and Come bettors clean up when 7 takes a recess, the laws of probability continue to operate. The more bets the player has on the table at one time, the more rapidly the percentage takes effect. Eventually, losses on Come tax the lover of all-out action most severely. Most readers will be happiest with a bet on Pass plus a maximum of one bet on Come immediately after the shooter rolls a come-out point.

DON'T COME

This relates to Come as Don't Pass does to Pass. The Don't Come bettor can lay odds (risking a good deal of money against a remarkably low combined vigorish). Also, the player can take off the odds or totally withdraw a Don't Come bet at any time, which is just as bad an idea as canceling a Don't Pass bet.

TWO PLACE BETS

Before any roll, a player is permitted to bet that a particular box number (4, 5, 6, 8, 9, or 10) will appear before 7 does. Two of these Place bets, as they are known, involve a vig of only 1.5 percent each. These are the bets on 6 or 8. When either wins, the house pays at the rate of $7 for every $6 that has been wagered. Thus, at tables with the increasingly familiar $5 minimum, one stakes $30 and, if lucky, gets back $65, including the $35 in winnings. At the opposite extreme, tables with 25-cent minimums will accept Place bets of $1.50 on 6 or 8, returning $3.25 to the victorious.

In 1977, the inaugural issue of the Las Vegas bimonthly, *Casino & Sports*, reported the fascinating 6–8 method of a gambler reputed to win $200 a day by placing both 6 and 8 at 25-cent tables, using a steep Great Martingale progression. Inasmuch as 6 and 8 can be made in ten ways and 7 in only six ways, chances are good that *either* a 6 or 8 will turn up before 7 does. Naturally, when 7 appears, both the Place bets are lost. But when either 6 or 8 shows, the one number wins and the other bet is unaffected. The gambler in question always withdrew the unaffected bet after winning the other one, and then launched a new series with $1.50 on each number. Playing that way reduced the vigorish to 1.04 percent.

The Martingale progression was so severe that, on the sixth bet of the series, the gambler was wagering $243 on each number in hope of catching one of the numbers and netting a profit of $1.50 on the series. A loss on the sixth bet would have made the total loss on the series $1,011. But the man claimed never to have lost six bets in succession and also declared that he was making his $200 a day in about two hours of betting. The magazine observed that the odds against hitting six 7's before encountering a single 6 or 8 were 359–1, which gave that resourceful gambler a real edge over the game—at least until the absolutely inevitable day when the 7's began to do their dirty work. Indeed, over a longer period of time than the gambler had tested the system, the probabilities dictated frequent enough losses to produce a net deficit of $180 per week!

I go into all this because it is interesting and because straight Place betting on 6 or 8 or both incurs a low house take, is exceedingly simple, and may appeal to some readers.

101

INADVISABLE BETS

We have finished our discussion of the only bets worth making at a Craps table. For information purposes, we now describe sucker propositions with which casinos inflate their advantage over unwary gamblers. In each case, the enticement is the possibility of a liberal payoff if the bet wins. But the payoff never is as liberal as it seems. I hope that the reader will concentrate on the Craps bets already reviewed, avoiding all that follow.

Other Place Bets: We have seen that Place bets on 6 and 8 involve a vig of only 1.5 percent. Similar bets also are available on 4, 5, 9, and/or 10. If 4 or 10 appears before 7 does, the house pays 9–5 (as contrasted with the proper odds of 2–1). And if 5 or 9 materializes before 7, the house pays 7–5, instead of the proper 3–2. The vig on 4 or 10 is 6.6 percent. On 5 or 9, it is 4 percent.

Buy Bets: In some casinos, it is possible to get proper odds on 4, 5, 6, 8, 9, or 10 by "buying" the number for a "commission" of 5 percent. The betting procedure is exactly like Place betting, except that the player hands over the prescribed number of extra chips when buying. For example, to buy a $20 bet on 9 would cost $21. The house edge is 4.8 percent. If a player wants to bet that a 7 will appear before one of the point numbers does, and lay the

102

odds, a so-called Lay bet also costs 5 percent and, depending on the number bet against, reaps the house 2.4 to 4 percent.

Big 6 and Big 8: We have already noted that a Place bet on 6 or 8 is not a bad deal. Nevertheless, the typical Craps layout contains a conspicuously situated area for bets on Big 6 or Big 8, which pay even money (1–1) when the desired number appears before a 7 does. The house drags down 9 percent. Need I observe that anyone who plays Big 6 or Big 8 demonstrates total helplessness?

Field Bets: On the players' side of the Come area is the Field box, which usually displays the numbers 2, 3, 4, 9, 10, 11, and 12, although sometimes a 5 replaces the 4. The player bets that the next roll will produce any field number. If that happens, the house pays 1–1. This is particularly pernicious, giving the house 11 percent. Uninformed gamblers find it especially attractive, since they have seven numbers going for them, and can lose on only four. Alas, the seven winning numbers can be made in 16 ways, but the four losing numbers are made in 20. Some casinos make the proposition more attractive by paying 2–1 on 2 and 12, or 2–1 on one and 3–1 on the other. This reduces the vig to 5.3 or 2.6 percent, no bargains.

Hardway Bets: A 4, 6, 8, or 10 is said to be rolled the

hard way when the dice come up 2–2, 3–3, 4–4, or 5–5, respectively. The hardway number must appear not only before a 7 does but before the desired number is produced by an unwanted combination. Thus, a hardway 8 bet loses if the dice land 5–3. Hard 4 or 10 pays 7–1 for a house edge of 11 percent. Hard 6 or 8 pays 9–1, with a 9 percent vig.

Hop Hardway: Now the hardway number must turn up on the next roll, a 35–1 shot that usually pays only 30–1, for a house percentage of 14.

Other Hop Bets: In many casinos, a player can bet that any two-way number will appear on the next toss. The most popular of these propositions are 3, 11, and any individual combination that produces 7 (6–1, 5–2, or 4–3). Each pays 15–1 for a vig of 11 percent. Some places pay only 14–1, raising the percentage to 16.6.

Any Craps: Wins if the next roll is 2, 3, or 12, paying 7–1 for an 11 percent vig.

Any 7: Another one-roller, paying 4–1 (16.6 percent for the house) or 9–2 (8.3 percent).

Craps 2 or Craps 12: Indistinguishable from hardway bets, the proper odds against each of which are 35–1.

These two usually pay from 29–1 to 32–1, yielding vigs of 8.3 to 16.6 percent.

Horn: For not less than four times the table's minimum bet, the chump can wager that the next throw will come up 2, 3, 11, or 12. Payoffs vary from as low as 4–1 to whatever odds would be paid if the winning number had been bet singly on the hop. Where the higher odds prevail, the house pays off on only the victorious fourth of the original bet, confiscating the losing three-quarters. This increases the already exorbitant vigorish on one-roll bets involving 2, 3, 11, or 12. Where the payoff is 4–1, it is paid on the total amount of the original bet, for a vig of almost 17 percent.

Note: The terms of their employment require stickmen and dealers to treat ignorant customers with blandly courteous cruelty, encouraging bets most favorable to the house and then, when a pigeon actually wins on one of the dreadful one-roll propositions, dawdling about the payoff. For example, the help in many casinos automatically refrain from returning the original chips to someone who has won a Hop or similar bet. They merely push the winnings across and let the original bet ride for a repeat, as if rendering the customer a big favor. On the other hand, dealers do not horse around with more intelligent gamblers. In fact, they usually are attentively helpful to anyone, regardless of inexperience, who seeks information or other

assistance for the purpose of placing low-vig bets. During
a win streak and most certainly at the end of a session in
which the table help has been pleasant, it is good form to
hand a chip or two to the stickman, who is collector for the
entire crew. Some big swingers do not tip directly, but hand
the stickman some chips and order a bet for the crew,
usually on the 11.

SUMMARY

STRATEGY FOR BEGINNERS

While becoming accustomed to all the hullabaloo, make
small bets on Pass or Don't Pass. If you do not feel equal
to handling the dice, decline the role of shooter when your
turn comes up. The stickman will then push the cubes to
the player at your left.

After you begin to feel more at ease, try an Anti-
Martingale with a two-bet paroli on Pass or Don't Pass. Or,
if you are ready for the slight extra concentration, launch
Oscar's Grind on one or the other.

STRATEGY FOR INTERMEDIATES

If you know the house rules and the true odds, you might
want to try two-bet parolis both on Pass and on supplementary bets at free odds. The arithmetic on a Free Odds

paroli can become confusing, since it is not always possible to bet the entire proceeds of one winning bet on the second half of the series. To make things simple, keep the chips from the winning free-odds bet in a separate place before you on the rim of the table and, when the time comes for the second half of that paroli, bet whatever portion of the stack the dealer will accept. Or, if ahead of the game and feeling adventurous, add a few chips to make a larger bet. To understand why this may be necessary or desirable, review the section "Pass Plus Free Odds" (page 92).

STRATEGY FOR VETERANS

If you feel energetic, you may enjoy operating separate grinds or parolis on both Pass and Come. Especially cool customers will even be able to take free odds on both, using separate pockets and/or stacks of chips sequestered on the table rim for bookkeeping purposes. Other entertaining combinations are Don't Pass and Come, or Pass and Don't Come. But laying off free odds on the Don't bets is not recommended. Ties up too much capital.

Some gamblers may find it more relaxing and every bit as much fun to run separate grinds or parolis while making Place bets on 6 and 8.

The experienced will bear in mind, I hope, that, while spreading relatively small bets around the table intensifies excitement, it heightens the effect of the house percentage.

In the long run, bets on a single deal such as Pass plus Free Odds minimize the house's advantage and, with canny money management and an occasional run of luck, produce superior results.

FOUR:
BACCARAT

MOST VERSIONS OF THIS REMARKABLE CARD GAME ARE surpassingly easy to play and offer gamblers the unusual opportunity to win about half of their bets. Naturally, there are catches. The first and less important is atmospheric: As presented in most casinos, the game is fraught with pomp, such as tuxedoed dealers, playing areas bounded by velvet ropes, and ceremonious table procedures that retard the action and prolong the suspense but are absolutely irrelevant to the outcome of bets. A stronger deterrent is the cost of play. On busy evenings in major American casinos, the minimum Baccarat wager is $20, with maximums $2,000 or higher. At European resorts, the scale is even more forbidding. For those well-heeled enough to play it, Baccarat in almost any form is the purest and fairest of casino pastimes, and an opportunity to test one's favorite betting plan against a house advantage of less than 1.2 percent.

THE BASIC PROCEDURES

In all kinds of Baccarat, each bet depends on the outcome of a point-count showdown between two hands of

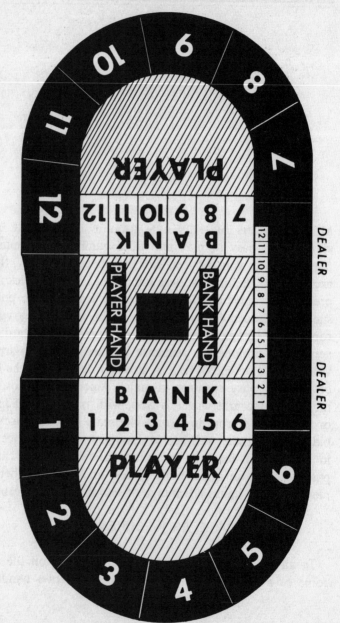

BACCARAT LAYOUT

two or three cards each. One of the hands is known as that of the Banker. The other is that of the Player or, in some constituencies, the Punter. In most versions, the gamblers never touch the cards and have nothing to do with the play of the hands, which are dealt and played by a house dealer according to strict rules. Where the customer actually handles cards, participation is a mere formality and takes place under close supervision. In the few versions that pit players against each other rather than against the house, the person whose turn it is to be Banker and the opponent who has won the right to be Player may actually exercise options in the play of their hands. But the options are limited and have absolutely no effect on the probabilities of the game. At most Baccarat tables, then, the house staff attends to everything. The players are spectators who bet. To bet, they usually are required to occupy a seat at the table, although some places allow standees to bet in partnership with seated players.

As noted, the hands are compared in terms of points. In keeping with the sappy traditions that lend the game its air, picture cards and tens do not count but are included in the six- or eight-deck packs and are dealt as if they mattered. Other cards count at face value from 1 (the Ace) to 9. Finally, if the sum of two countable cards is 10 or higher, the first digit is ignored and the point value is that of the second digit. For example, a hand of 7 and 8 counts 15 at face value but is worth only 5. And a 6 and 4 becomes 0.

A point count of 8 or 9 wins unless tied by the opposing hand. Nobody wins or loses on ties. If neither hand totals 8 or 9, the winning hand is the one with the higher count of 7 or less.

All winning bets pay even money—a dollar won for each dollar risked. In most American versions, the gambler is free to bet on either Banker or Player as the spirit moves, and the entire proceedings are conducted under inflexible rules that relieve the customer of all burdens except those of money management.

The main varieties are:

Nevada Baccarat: When played with a British-Latino vocabulary, this is known as Baccarat Punto Banco. It is entirely mechanical and, like Craps or Roulette, could be programmed into electronic slot machines. The customers gamble against the house, betting as they please on Banker or Player.

Mini-Baccarat is the same game without the folderol. At a small table not unlike a Blackjack layout, one dealer serves up the two contending hands. Play is even faster than at Craps and, where available in Nevada, offers much lower betting minimums than are necessitated by more formal versions with larger table crews.

Chemin de Fer finds the gamblers betting against each

other rather than against the house. One of the customers serves as Banker and bets on that hand. Rules vary in rigidity from place to place. In the traditional game, and unlike Nevada Baccarat, both Player and Banker have occasional options about whether to draw a third card. The Banker may also be required to stake all proceeds of each previous winning bet on the next bet, or yield up the bank.

Baccarat en Banque invites the customer to bet on either of two Player hands dispensed by a house dealer, who plays the Banker hand. Unhampered by the strictures that govern other forms of the game, the house dealer may draw a third card or stand on the original two. That decision invariably depends on the dealer's expert estimate of how best to defeat the Player hand on which the larger amount has been wagered. This is no pastime for the modestly funded or inexperienced.

THE PERCENTAGES

A superbly detailed booklet called *The Facts of Baccarat*, by Walter I. Nolan, is published for $1 by Gambler's Book Club (see Appendix A), and is worth many times the price. Nolan shows that, since tied hands neither profit nor penalize those who bet on Banker or Player, a gambler who backs the Banker hand at Nevada Baccarat or Punto Banco should win about 50.68 percent of those bets. Bets on Player win about 49.32 percent. These expectations produce a house percentage of 1.17 against Banker and 1.36 against Player. The explanation follows:

The house advantage on Player bets consists of the fact that the casino beats Player 50.68 percent of the time. Losing to Banker that same percentage of the time and paying promptly at the prescribed even money, the house recovers its edge by charging each winning Banker bettor a 5 percent commission—25 cents for each $5 in winnings. Needless to add, many casinos charge the full 25 cents on each $5 or *fraction* thereof, inflating the commission and the house advantage. Canny players circumvent this by asking floor personnel what the house practices are and tailoring their Banker bets to hold the house commission to a minimum.

Some casinos offer 8–1 odds to customers willing to bet that the next hand will produce a tie. The house edge on this is about 14.1 percent, a preposterous waste of money.

Vigorish at Chemin de Fer and Baccarat en Banque tends to be even lower than that of Nevada Baccarat. In Chemin de Fer, the role of Banker rotates among the players at the table. The house sometimes does not collect its commission after each winning hand, as in the Nevada game, but may await the conclusion of a Banker's turn and base its commission on that customer's net winnings, if any, for the entire turn. When the Banker ends a loser, the house gets nothing. It also gets nothing from the other players, whose losses become the property of the gambler who happens to be Banker at the time. And in Baccarat en Banque, a smart tactician who tries to confine bets to the Player hand that has attracted less betting support may by that means reduce the house take, winning somewhat more frequently than would be possible otherwise. As observed earlier about Baccarat en Banque, the house dealer tends to place major emphasis on beating the Player hand on which more money has been wagered.

THE DEAL (NEVADA AND PUNTO BANCO)

In Baccarat en Banque and Mini-Baccarat, customers never deal. In Nevada Baccarat and Punto Banco, although the gamblers also play against the house and not against each other, an opportunity to deal the cards rotates among them. Apparently this fortifies enjoyment, possibly because gamblers like to feel somehow instrumental in the proceedings. So the Nevada Baccarat client is called "dealer" for as many turns as it takes to produce a winning Player hand, whereupon the deal moves counterclockwise to the adjoining customer. At Punto Banco, the player who deals the cards is called *curator*. Each dispenses the previously shuffled and cut cards from a dealing box, or *shoe*, under the hawk-eyed supervision of a house dealer, placing cards where that functionary directs and exposing them as instructed. In short, the role of curator or dealer is entirely meaningless and contributes nothing to the game that could not be accomplished more expeditiously by a house employee. Players who do not wish to participate in the dealing ritual are allowed to abstain.

All bets are made before the deal begins. Persons who want to bet on Player put their chips directly in front of them in the layout space marked "Player." Those who bet on Banker reach slightly farther, using boxed areas marked with the numbers that identify their positions at the table.

Under house direction, the two cards of the Player hand usually are placed face down near the customer who has bet the largest amount on that hand. The Banker cards may at first go face down beneath the shoe. Practices of this kind vary and are of no consequence. Sooner or later the dumb show ceases, the casino's caller turns the cards (or directs the dealer and a player to do so), and play begins. Play consists of the caller deciding on the basis of the rules whether the Player hand gets a third card and, after that, whether the Banker hand draws or stands. The rules of the draw are inflexible. Unfortunately, they usually are presented (on posters or small cards) in a lamentably confusing tabular form. Although the table caller and other members of the staff know the rules by heart and enforce them honestly (in most places), the customer deserves information more intelligible than the gibberish printed on the cards handed out at casinos. Especially at $20 a hand.

Here are the rules:

1. The Player hand always stands on a two-card total of 6 to 9.

2. Unless the Banker hand shows a *natural* 8 or 9, the Player hand always gets a third card when the value of its first two cards is 0 to 5.

3. Nothing is done about the Banker hand until it has been determined whether the Player hand stands or, if required, a third card has been added to the Player hand.

4. With a two-card count of 0, 1, or 2, the Banker hand always gets a third card, unless the Player hand shows a winning 8 or 9.

5. With a two-card count of 7, 8, or 9, the Banker hand always stands, getting no third card.

6. With a two-card count of 3, 4, 5, or 6, the Banker hand sometimes gets a third card and sometimes does not. It all depends on (a) whether the Player hand has been given a third card and (b) the value of the Player hand's third card, if any. Here is what the rules provide in these cases:

a. If the Player hand gets no third card, the Banker hand must stand on a two-card total of 6, and must draw on a two-card total of 3, 4, or 5.

b. If the Player gets a third card, the Banker hand stands or draws as follows:

BANKER HOLDS	STANDS WHEN PLAYER'S THIRD CARD IS	DRAWS WHEN PLAYER'S THIRD CARD IS
3	0 to 7, 9	8
4	2 to 7	0, 1, 8, 9
5	4 to 7	0 to 3; 8, 9
6	6 or 7	0 to 5; 8, 9

All that having been attended to, the house pays the backers of whatever hand totals 9, or closer thereto. In ties, nobody wins. And, of course, if either or both hands began with a natural 8 or 9, the decision is reached more quickly.

THE DEAL (CHEMIN DE FER)

After the cards have been shuffled and deposited in the shoe, the customer who offers to bet the largest amount on the first hand becomes the Banker, takes the shoe under the supervision of the caller, and prepares to play the Banker hand. In case two offer to bet the same amount, the customer nearer to the caller (counterclockwise) becomes Banker.

Having become Banker on a high bid, the customer is required to bet at least as much as the bid. As soon as that wager is placed, other players have the opportunity to cover all or part of that amount with bets of their own on the opposing Player hand.

A gambler who wants to cover the entire amount of the Banker's bet signifies this by calling, "Banco." If such a player loses that bet and wants first priority to cover the whole of the Banker's bet on the next hand, the call is "Banco Suivi" or "Suivi." If nobody calls "Suivi" and two or more offer "Banco," the privilege goes to the player seated closer to the caller, moving counterclockwise. And if nobody calls "Banco," each player at the table is given an opportunity to cover part of the bet, beginning with the player immediately to the right of the Banker and proceeding counterclockwise. After the entire amount of the bet has been covered, or, failing that, after all players have had their opportunity to bet on the Player hand against the Banker, the caller announces, "No more bets," and the actual deal begins.

Formalities require that the player with the largest bet control the Player's hand (under firm guidance by a dealer, of course).

The rules of the deal are identical with those of Nevada Baccarat, with these exceptions:

1. With a two-card total of 5, the Player may either draw a third card or stand with the original holding. It makes no difference as far as the percentages of the game are concerned.

2. With a two-card total of 3, and having dealt the Player a 9 as a third card, the Banker may elect to stand or draw. It makes no difference.

3. With a two-card total of 5, and having dealt the Player a 4 as a third card, the Banker again has the option of standing or drawing. It makes no difference.

As played in the United States, Chemin de Fer rules usually permit the Banker to withdraw winnings after each successful hand, and continue at the level of the original bet. Elsewhere, the Banker may be required to leave all winnings on the table, parlaying the bets. In some places, the Banker is allowed to withdraw winnings but continue as Banker after two or three successive victories. And, in any casino, a Banker may give up the bank at any time. When that happens, a new auction may be held or the bank may simply pass to the player at the retiring Banker's right, just as it does when a Banker loses a hand.

In Europe, the caller is known as *croupier*, and the game is conducted in French:

Sabot: The dealing shoe.

Banquier: Banker.

Associé: A standee who bets as the Banker's partner, not widely permitted in America.

Avec la table: A proposal by a player to bet "with the table"—an amount at least half of the Banker's full wager.

Rien ne va plus: "No more bets."

Huit: Eight.

Neuf: Nine.

Carte: "Card"—a request that a card be dealt.

Non: "No"—meaning that no third card is wanted.

BETTING STRATEGY

The very best bets at Craps are somewhat more likely to lose than to win. Baccarat presents more favorable possibilities. Banker is more likely to win than to lose, and Player is almost as likely to win as to lose. For practical purposes, the situation is comparable to an honestly conducted coin-flipping game of Heads and Tails in which Heads (call it Banker) agrees to pay the owner of the coin five cents of every dollar won, while Tails (call it Player) is allowed to keep all winnings. The fact that Player operates under a statistical disadvantage over the long term is not very relevant to short-term play. In a contest of 10 million Baccarat hands, for example, Banker should win about 136,000 more than Player, ruining the poor soul. But in 100 hands, Banker's statistical advantage is less than a hand-and-a-half, allowing Player a good chance of ending considerably ahead without stretching the laws of probability even a little bit.

Carrying this further, if Banker finishes a 100-hand Nevada Baccarat session with 51 victories to Player's 49, and if the table has a $5 minimum, a bettor on Banker goes home a loser. The Banker hand won 51 times, grossing $255, but lost 49 times, returning $245. But the Banker bettor paid the house 25 cents for each of the 51 winning hands—$12.75, abolishing the $10 profit and then some. But if Player had won 51 hands, which should have surprised nobody, that gambler's $10 profit would have remained intact. At many European Chemin de Fer tables, of course, Banker pays a house commission only on the net winnings of each turn, and in the situation just described might have ended ahead, having won some hands as Player between turns with the shoe.

All this is meant to imply that the various Baccarats are so nearly even propositions that the casino gambler can safely ignore the long-range probabilities and bet Banker or Player in random patterns while depending on Oscar's Grind or an Anti-Martingale to capitalize on whatever advantages the cards may supply.

Most of the playing systems favored by Baccarat fiends seek to anticipate hoped-for rhythmical shifts between wins for Player and wins for Banker. As the attentive reader already must know, casino games cooperate with these grand designs only by accident. One of the most familiar systems of the kind is called *Avant Dernier*, which is French for "before last." The gambler bets on whatever side won the next-to-last hand. Absolutely nothing is wrong with this approach, except when adopted by someone who assumes that it is uniquely effective. In truly random games like this, any approach is as good as any other.

The leisurely pace of all Baccarat games except Mini-Baccarat gives even an inexperienced gambler ample time for mental arithmetic. Elaborate combinations of Anti-Martingale parolis become more practical here than in the hectic atmosphere of Craps. For example, the gambler might begin each betting series as both a two-bet and three-bet paroli. Beginning with a bet of two units, the gambler lets the four chips ride after the first successful bet. If this second bet wins, the gambler withdraws four units, letting the other four ride. If that third bet wins, the procedure begins all over again, a profit of 10 units having been pocketed. Note that if the second bet wins and the third loses, the undertaking nets a profit of two units. Players with larger capital and stronger appetites can extend this principle considerably, operating numerous ongoing parolis at once and profiting greatly when a winning streak for Banker or Player reaches the fourth or fifth successive win.

FIVE:
BLACKJACK

THIS LIVELY CARD GAME, KNOWN ALSO AS TWENTY-ONE or Vingt-et-Un, differs significantly from other casino attractions. Although the customers bet as usual against the house and not against each other, the rules allow them to employ tactics which actually affect the outcome of their bets. At all other gaming tables worth considering, your tactics begin and end with bet selection and money management. Once you've placed your bet, the outcome depends entirely on chance. But a Blackjack player may stand with a two-card hand or draw additional cards in an informed effort to beat the house and reduce its income.

Depending on house rules, which vary from place to place and are always subject to abrupt change, a skillful player manipulates the probabilities of the game successfully enough to lower the vigorish to an average of about 1.5 percent. Indeed, where rules are most lenient, Blackjack becomes an approximately even game for the educated player. As we shall see, certain enterprising and extremely gifted sharks have contrived to shift the ad-

BLACKJACK LAYOUT

BLACKJACK
pays 3 to 2
DEALER MUST STAND ON 17 AND DRAW TO 16
INSURANCE PAYS 2 TO 1

vantage even further to the player's side, making the game unfavorable to the house. Casinos detest shenanigans of that kind. More later.

RULES AND PROCEDURES

Because it is a card game of point counts and showdowns, Blackjack seems at first to resemble Baccarat. The differences are great. Most notably, the Blackjack customer's right to stand on the original hand or draw additional cards is unlimited by Baccarat-style rules. Each player has a separate hand. Each deal is a competition between the house dealer's hand and the individual holdings played by the six or seven gamblers accommodated at a table.

The player's object is a point count higher than that held by the dealer, but not higher than 21. A player or dealer with 22 points or more has *busted* and loses.

An Ace counts 1 or 11, as the player pleases. In practice, it is counted as 11 unless to do so raises the point count above 21.

The numbered cards (2 through 10), count at face value.

Picture cards count 10 points each.

Suits and colors are ignored.

Before each deal, the players make their bets, placing chips in spaces clearly marked at each seating position on the table layout. The dealer then dispenses one card at a time, clockwise, beginning with the customer at the far right end of the player's side of the table. Depending on casino policy and prevailing demand, the dealer works with a pack of from one to as many as eight decks, sliding the cards out of a dealing box (shoe) when using a pack of three decks or more. In some places, the players get their two-card hands face up, elsewhere face down. The face-down custom creates suspense but makes no other difference. The dealer always gets one exposed card. The other may be dealt face down before actual play begins or may be withheld until time to play the house hand, whereupon it is dealt face up.

A player with 21 in the first two cards (an Ace with a 10 or any picture card) has Blackjack and is paid at odds of 3–2 unless the dealer also gets Blackjack, a situation known as a *push* or tie, which the Blackjack-holding player neither wins nor loses. A player who gets Blackjack exposes the hand immediately, if the cards were not dealt face up.

After all the players have seen their original two-card holdings, the dealer faces the player at the extreme right of the table (to the dealer's left) and begins the next phase, in which players who want additional cards are given their opportunity, by turns. Where the first two cards are dealt face down, the approved signal for a *hit* (another card) is transmitted by lifting the original hand slightly (still face down) and brushing the edges of the cards toward oneself on the table surface. One or two such motions suffice. Some players prefer to say, "Hit me," or simply beckon with a forefinger. The player is entitled to as many hits as may seem useful. Each additional card arrives face up. When satisfied that the hand has achieved a desirable (or at least practical) point total, the player signifies a readiness to *stand* by slipping the original face-down cards under the chips that represent the bet.

Where all cards are dealt face upward, the wish for a hit is usually a beckoning gesture or the words, "Hit me." And the desire to stand is conveyed by a sideways, palm-down "all done" motion. Casinos that deal Blackjack with all cards exposed usually expect players to conduct their business without touching the cards.

A player who has busted (taken one card too many for a total of more than 21 points) is expected to expose the hand at once, if the cards were not already face upward in the deal. A player who has busted is an immediate loser, even though the dealer may later bust the house hand.

After all the players have finished drawing and standing or busting, the dealer either exposes the house's down card or deals that hand a second exposed card and, if the rules require, takes additional cards. The dealer has no options. In any decent casino, the dealer always draws to a hand worth 16 points or less, and always stands on 17 points or more. Furthermore, the stand-on-17 rule is interpreted in such establishments as applying to a two-card holding of an Ace plus any other card worth 6 or more—meaning that in those circumstances the dealer does not have the option of regarding the Ace as a 1-point card.

Having completed play with a bust for the house, the dealer pays off at even money to players who did not bust and at 3–2 to players holding Blackjack. Not having busted, but with a point count of 17 or more, the dealer pays off players who survived the play of their own hands without busting and ended with point counts higher than that of the house hand. The dealer collects from those with lower point counts, and picks up the cards but does not touch the chips of players whose hands tied the house's. If the dealer has a Blackjack, the house beats any hand with 21 points but three or more cards.

ADDITIONAL PLAYS

Doubling Down: A player with a two-card count of 8, 9, 10, or 11 may like the idea of doubling the original bet in hope of drawing a 10 or a picture as third card in a powerful holding. To signify readiness for this play, the gambler places the additional chips alongside those of the original bet. If the hand was not exposed on the deal, its two cards are now faced overlapping lengthwise, and the dealer serves a third card face down. No additional cards are allowed. Where the original cards are dealt face up and the player is supposed to keep hands off, a desire to

DOUBLING DOWN

double down is communicated verbally. In some casinos, doubling down is allowed only on a two-card count of 9, 10, or 11. Some places do not accept doubles on 9. And some require only that the original bet be increased, not necessarily doubled.

Splitting Pairs: Holding two cards of equal denomination in the original hand, a player may choose to separate them, using each as the beginning of a hand. Facing them upward and placing them parallel to but apart from each other in the playing area, the gambler moves the original bet behind one of them and puts an equal number of chips behind the other. If the cards are Aces, the dealer then completes the process by placing a single card on each. With a pair of any other denomination, as many additional cards may be drawn to each hand as the player wants. In some casinos, if the first card drawn to one of the new hands is of the same denomination as the first pair, that card may be used to start a third hand. And when the dealer's hand turns out to be a Blackjack, some casinos collect only the original bet from the chips played by a pair-splitter, returning the extra ones that were stakes for splitting. In casinos that deal the original hands face upward, players use words to request doubling down.

Insurance: When the dealer's exposed card (in some places, first card) is an Ace, players are invited to make

SPLITTING A PAIR

insurance bets. Risking at least half the amount of the original bet, the player wins the insurance bet at odds of 2–1 when the dealer's second card is worth 10 points, giving the house a Blackjack.

Surrender: An increasing number of casinos permit players to retrieve half of the wagered amount when they do not like their first two cards and decide to surrender before trying a third card. In some establishments, surrender is permitted with a hand of three cards.

THE HOUSE ADVANTAGE

The casino's principal edge is the rule that allows it to win on a player's busted hand *before* the dealer has confronted the house's own hand and, as happens, has exposed it to the risk of additional cards and a possible bust. In his authoritative *The Casino Gambler's Guide*, Dr. Allan N. Wilson says that this privilege supplies the house an advantage of almost 7 percent. But the 3–2 odds paid on Blackjack reduce the vigorish to about 4.5 percent. Correct playing tactics—combined with the rule that permits the dealer no tactics but requires that the house hit with 16 and stand on 17 or more—serve to pare the house edge enough to make Blackjack a virtually even game for any player who confines play to more generous casinos and knows a few simple tactics.

EFFECTIVE PLAY

Unlike Roulette and Craps, whose cut-and-dried probabilities have been understood for centuries, Blackjack developed by guess and by gosh. The first solid information about the percentages of the game began emerging from the computers of various mathematicians shortly after mid-century. Many of these playful scholars, such as Edward O. Thorp, Allan N. Wilson, Julian Braun, and Roger Baldwin, learned vastly more about the game than any casino management had ever dreamed of. Some, like Thorp, made fortunes at the tables and taught others how to follow suit. It took the gambling industry several years to realize that something was afoot.

What follows here is a fairly simple playing strategy that originated in the writings of the mathematicians named above and has become standard among Blackjack enthusiasts who would rather win than lose. At best, this strategy places the player on an even footing with the house, meaning that when the cards fall favorably, the informed player who practices sensible money management can win many short sessions. Measures taken by some casinos to assure themselves a clear advantage will be dealt with below. Here are the basic tactics:

Hard Hands: These are hands in which no Aces appear or, if present, are valued at 1 point each.

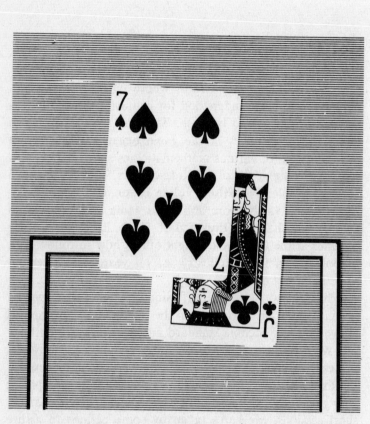

HARD 17

WHEN DEALER'S EXPOSED CARD IS	PLAYER DRAWS WHEN HOLDING
2 or 3	12 or less
4, 5, or 6	11 or less
7 or higher	16 or less
OTHERWISE PLAYER STANDS	

Soft Hands: When counting an Ace as 11:

WHEN DEALER'S EXPOSED CARD IS	PLAYER DRAWS WHEN HOLDING
A to 8	17 or less
9 or higher	18 or less

Doubling Down: Double the bet whenever the original hand totals 11. When holding 10, double only if the dealer shows neither a 10-point card nor an Ace. With a count of 9, double only when the dealer shows 6 or less. Players who can tolerate extra complications can do so to their advantage by doubling down when holding a *soft* 13, 14, 15, or 16 (A–2, A–3, A–4, A–5) against a dealer who shows a 4, 5, or 6. With a soft 17 or 18, doubling down is recommended against a dealer with 3, 4, 5, or 6.

Splitting Pairs: Always split Aces and eights. Never split fives or tens. In fact, the new player should confine splits to Aces and eights until ready to absorb some of

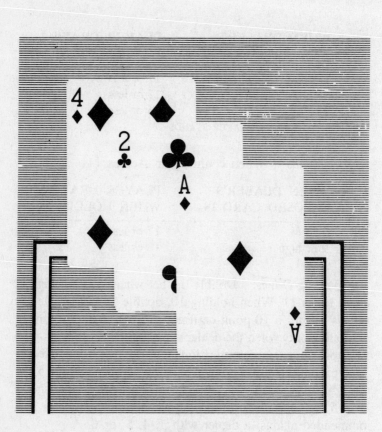

SOFT 17

the advanced plays set forth in the writings of Edward O. Thorp, Allan N. Wilson, and Julian Braun.

Insurance: This is a sucker bet, on which the house has an advantage of almost 6 percent.

Surrender: Julian Braun has processed this comparatively recent innovation and has reported in various publications of Gambler's Book Club that it is advantageous to surrender hands of 10–5 and 9–6 when the dealer shows a ten. When the dealer's exposed card is an Ace, a holding of 10–6 should be tossed in. Otherwise, the surrender option gets into the realm of the exotic, depending on advanced knowledge of infinitesimal percentage changes attributable to the number of decks in the dealer's pack. In the few places that permit surrender of a three-card or larger hand, it is advisable to abandon ship when the count of the first three or more cards is 15 or 16 against a dealer who shows a ten.

OBSTACLES

The basic strategy is most effective at a table where the dealer uses only one deck of cards, the player is permitted all possible options on splitting pairs or doubling down, and the dealer is subject to the traditional rules in hitting the house hand. The tourist may occasionally find a casino which recognizes no pushes, confiscating the player's bet even after a tie. This represents a house advantage of approximately 9 percent, and should promptly repel the prudent. So should refusal by a casino to permit doubling down on a point count of 10, which is worth about .5 percent, or on 11, which is worth about .8 percent. Where four decks are used, the house advantage is about .4 percent larger than in the one-deck game.

CARD COUNTING

Early in the 1960s, a book called *Beat the Dealer*, by Dr. Edward O. Thorp, inflamed the avarice of gamblers everywhere. The book told how to make Blackjack a game unfavorable to the casino—a sure thing for the customer. Thorp had already tested the approach in actual casino play. Much of the book was an elated summary of his own victories, which had enriched him.

The operating principle was easy to understand, but its application was enormously difficult. Basic strategy, explained Thorp, was most valid for the first hand dealt after a shuffle and cut. As cards were dealt, the deck's composition was altered and so were the probabilities on which sound tactics depended. Therefore, it was important to keep track of the changing character of the deck by noticing which cards were dealt and, by subtraction, which cards remained to be dealt. Thorp was good at that. As the deck dwindled, he not only modified his decisions on hitting or standing but, even more important, modified the size of his bets. When the deck was rich in high-point cards favorable to the player but likely to force the dealer into a bust, he happily multiplied his bets.

It took the gambling industry years to agree that Thorp and his growing legion of card counters or "casedowners" could really beat the game. The industry's counteroffensive took many forms, the mildest of which included dealing from four decks or more instead of one and reshuffling before the shoe was half empty, or, in some places, shuffling after almost every hand. Many casinos discouraged card counters by throwing them out. A friend of mine was escorted from a Las Vegas casino to its parking lot, stuffed into the trunk of a car, taken to the airport, hustled onto an airplane, and advised not to return.

The card counters learned to cope with four-deck shoes. They learned to rent wigs, whiskers, and phony eyeglasses from theatrical costumers and to play incompetently before cashing a couple of big bets and vanishing. They learned to count cards without seeming to do so. Most recently, they learned to operate in teams, with the actual card counter never increasing the size of bets and, indeed, taking care to lose now and then. At the counter's signal, however, ostensibly inept confederates would suddenly make huge bets, win them, and depart.

Blackjack experts barred from play have sued the casinos

that discriminated against them, and have drawn support from individuals and organizations concerned with the preservation of civil liberties. Meanwhile, Blackjack has become by all accounts the most popular of the table games, with new generations of card counters completing their weeks of rehearsal and coming to the casinos by the hundreds, if not thousands. With rare exceptions, they lose. It takes talent bordering on genius and motivation on the threshold of monomania to track the characteristics of the cards remaining in a four-deck shoe. Casinos may have lost millions to the original counters and the few new experts that have followed in their footsteps, but I am quite sure that the industry has more than recouped those losses from other gamblers who can't count cards and, for that matter, can't master the game's basic strategy.

Card-counting systems have been published in great profusion, with the inventor of each claiming unprecedented advantage over helpless casino managements. Nonsense. The differences among results attainable with the various systems are microscopic and, in any event, the casinos are far from helpless. They now react so swiftly to the presence of even a mediocre casedown player that most experts have given up trying to penetrate the defenses.

My own attitude toward card counting comes in two parts. First, counting is a monumental waste of time for the average person whose desire to gamble does not extend beyond the recreational. Second, the casinos seem to me to have every right to frustrate the activities of persons who violate traditional ground rules. That is, the casinos are business enterprises which make their money on games unfavorable to customers. When wise guys come along and use slugs to drain the jackpots from slot machines, the casinos have every right to modify the machines. Similarly, they have a right to shuffle a Blackjack deck after every hand. Whether they have the right to toss card counters out on their ears is a matter for the courts, and is of no urgency to the gentle reader.

Persons whose curiosity has been aroused by all this talk of beating the casinos will find all the card-counting information they can possibly want in the Thorp book, Allan Wilson's book, and other materials sold by Gambler's Book Club. Details in Appendix A.

TOKING

Toward the end of a profitable encounter with a pleasant Blackjack dealer, it is good form to offer a tip. One elegant and highly acceptable procedure is to place a bet for the dealer—an extra number of chips placed between you and the dealer, usually on the arced area normally reserved for insurance bets. If you win the next hand, the dealer pockets the proceeds with thanks.

149

SIX:

SLOT MACHINES

ELECTRONIC CIRCUITRY HAS ADDED FLASHY ELABORATIONS to the old one-armed bandit without undermining its basic appeal—the opportunity to confront Lady Luck in virtual solitude, without embarrassment by complex rules, brusque dealers, other players, or, for that matter, one's own common sense. Countless thousands of gamblers never patronize a casino table. They head straight for the machines in the lobby—or even in the airport—and spend hour after hour in a state akin to trance, depositing more coins than they collect but coming away refreshed.

To play, you simply deposit a coin of the required denomination (from a nickel to a silver dollar to the multiple coins accepted by modern machines that increase the pay-offs in proportion to the amount of the bet, but do not increase the player's chances of winning). Having inserted the coin, you pull down the traditional handle on the right side of the apparatus. This activity causes three or more drums to revolve. When they come to rest, the visible surface of each displays a symbol. The pattern of the symbols

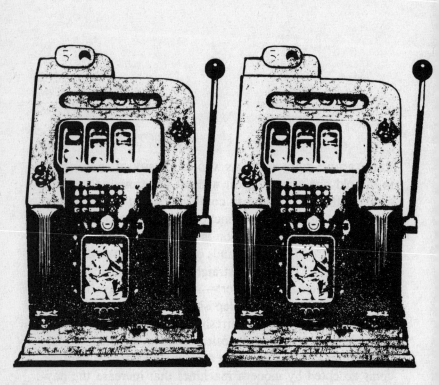

SLOT MACHINES

determines whether you have won, and how much. The winning patterns and the corresponding payoffs are clearly posted on the machine.

The highest aspiration of the player is the jackpot, an occurrence announced with flashing lights, loud bells, and coins cascading from the innards of the box. Some of the more elaborate machines offer jackpots of as much as $100,000. This means that the revolving drums do not often display the jackpot pattern. It also means that anybody who hits a jackpot of any size is well advised to assume that the money that fell from the machine was only part of the reward, the rest of which should be forthcoming from a casino employee.

The average bandit returns about 75 cents of every dollar—an outrageous house advantage of about 25 percent. Salted among them are others that take as little as 5 percent and are, therefore, a game as fair as Roulette. The difference, of course, is that the Roulette table is in plain view, its traditional percentages well known. But the occasional low-vig slot machine is a needle in a haystack. Assuming that the particular casino has some (which is far from certain), the gambler may expend many paper cups full of quarters or dimes or silver dollars without locating one of them. Or, having found one, the happy hunter will be playing a game five times as costly as smart Craps, routine Baccarat, or informed Blackjack.

According to a leading student of the slots, Jacques Noir,

Ph.D., low-vig machines are more likely to be found in Lake Tahoe or in downtown Las Vegas and Reno than in more prominent establishments.

I suppose that everybody should try the things for a while, simply for the strange experience. But do so in full expectation of losing, and do not be misled by an occasional success. Above all, do not try to apply any betting system. The house take is too large, and the machines operate entirely at random. As in any other casino game, the jackpot or some other payoff is never "due," no matter how the machine may have behaved during the previous half hour.

Much has been made of the warfare waged by allied casino operators and machine manufacturers against their guerrilla enemies—talented souls whose mission in life is to find a chink in the armor and walk off with all the jackpots. Over the years, the machines have been looted by a stupendous variety of means, ranging from hammers and screwdrivers and battery-operated drills to slugs, counterfeit coins, anti-static hair sprays that neutralized the circuitry, and a most particularly bright technique of determining a machine's timing accurately enough to make it stop on the desired jackpot at will. In due course, the casinos and manufacturers have nullified each of these brilliant manifestations of resourcefulness and initiative— improving the defenses, as it were. I have no doubt whatever that somewhere a college professor is experimenting with portable electronic devices to zap the machinery and get rich quick. How about a microwave beam projected from a vest button?

Honest persons who want to try the slots may benefit (but not greatly) from the fairly plausible supposition that a low-vig machine is unlikely to be situated next to anything but a high-vig machine. Having found one that seems to pay off more liberally than normal, it is best to concentrate on it rather than invest money in its near neighbors.

SEVEN:
KENO

THIS WESTERNIZED VERSION OF THE CELEBRATED CHINESE Lottery is like the Lotto of childhood or the Bingo still played, but more elaborate. Its details could fill half this book, but would not be worth the reader's time or my own. To rush to the heart of the matter, Keno gives the house an exorbitant edge of between 20 and 30 percent, depending on individual variations in the odds.

In other words, it is a miserably unfair game and nothing to risk serious money on. Beyond that, it offers certain creature comforts, including a place to sit (usually called the Keno lounge or parlor), a leisurely tempo, polite and helpful personnel, and sometimes free drinks. And it certainly provides suspense.

Before each game, the player gets a ticket that looks like its cousin, the Bingo ticket, except that it contains the numbers 1 through 80—all of them. Referring to the house list of payoffs, the player marks whatever number or combination of numbers strikes his fancy, and either takes the ticket and the money to a staff member called a "writer,"

✪KENO✪

$25,000.00

LIMIT EACH GAME

MARK PRICE HERE

WINNING TICKETS MUST BE COLLECTED IMMEDIATELY AFTER EACH GAME IS CALLED.

1	2	3	4	5	6	7	8	9	10
11	12	13	14	15	16	17	18	19	20
21	22	23	24	25	26	27	28	29	30
31	32	33	34	35	36	37	38	39	40

41	42	43	44	45	46	47	48	49	50
51	52	53	54	55	56	57	58	59	60
61	62	63	64	65	66	67	68	69	70
71	72	73	74	75	76	77	78	79	80

KENO RUNNERS ARE AVAILABLE FOR YOUR CONVENIENCE

KENO

or has a runner perform that duty. The writer validates the ticket, which is good for the next game only, and returns a copy to the player.

The game itself is a random process in which a machine called a *goose* blows twenty of eighty numbered plastic balls into two transparent tubes. As each ball materializes in a tube, its number is announced on a public-address system and also appears in lights on display boards in various parts of the casino. Obviously, if only 20 numbers turn up in a game, 60 do not. So the odds against the appearance of an individual number are 3–1. But the house pays only 2–1.

The player is allowed to bet on any of literally billions of different combinations of numbers. The simplest tickets are known as *spot* or *straight* tickets, on which the customer marks from one to fifteen numbers. When all the numbers marked on a 15-spot ticket actually come out of the goose, the lucky winner collects $25,000 for the 70-cent wager—unless, Lord preserve us, someone else hits at the same time, whereupon the prize is divided, lottery-style.

Somewhat more complicated than spot tickets are *way* tickets, which enable the player to combine on one sheet of paper what otherwise might occupy many separate spot tickets. For example, by circling the 5 and 15, the 20 and 29, and the 67 and 68, the player signifies a desire to bet that any two of the pairs enclosed in the three circles will appear. That is, the player wants a 3-way 4, a more convenient way to make a bet that also could be written on three different spot tickets: 5, 15, 20, 29; 5, 15, 67, 68; and 20, 29, 67, 68. Lovers of complication can bury themselves in way play, paying large sums for, let us say, 19 different three-number groups which combine themselves into 969 different 9-spot tickets.

The basic spot tickets offer a sliding scale of payoffs according to the number of marked numbers that appear on the board. Inasmuch as a way ticket is a combination of spot tickets, it may pay off in several ways at once. In the foregoing example, if 5, 15, 20, and 29 actually materialized, it would pay off twice—the second time for the 5 and 15 that were bet in combination with 67 and 68. To induce purchase of way tickets, some casinos cut the price per way to 35 cents.

Combinations even more exotic are available, with the help of any Keno writer. For example, the player may mark a ticket with various combinations of two numbers, three numbers, and four numbers, offering to play every possible result that can be formed by them. The writer always obliges.

This game has been excused on the ground that it offers bettors of modest means an opportunity to make lots of money for small investments. One can only comment that a lot of folks seem to love the pastime and that, in the long run, it probably costs them less than the slots do, because it takes longer.

EIGHT:
TRENTE-ET-QUARANTE

THIS EXCITING CARD GAME IS HIGHLY POPULAR IN THE casinos of France and Monte Carlo. It would be a logical addition to the American repertoire if floor space were not already cluttered with slot machines, Big Six wheels, Keno parlors, and other high-percentage grinds so dearly cherished by the industry.

Trente-et-Quarante is French for Thirty-and-Forty. The game also is known as *Rouge et Noir* (Red and Black). The house advantage is about 1.25 percent and in most places can be reduced by sensible play to a flat 1 percent.

Using a six-deck pack, the dealer (*tailleur*) deals a row of cards face upward until its point-count total exceeds 30. Aces count 1, pictures 10, and other cards are taken at face value. This first row of cards is known as Black (*Noir*).

Black having been dealt, the *tailleur* lays out a second row in exactly the same way, stopping when its value tops 30. This row is known as Red (*Rouge*).

The row with the lower point count wins for those who

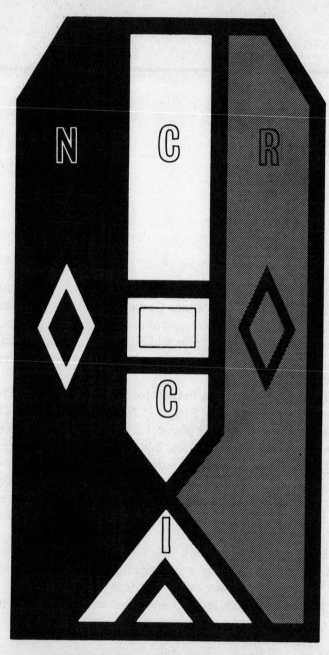

TRENTE-ET-QUARANTE LAYOUT

have bet on it. Naturally, all bets are made before the deal begins. Four different bets are accepted and pay the winners at even money:

1. *Noir.*
2. *Rouge.*
3. *Couleur*—a bet that the first card dealt to the *Black* row will be of the same color as the *winning* row. That is, if the first card dealt to Black is a Diamond and the Red row wins, a bet on *Couleur* also wins.
4. *Inverse*—a bet that the first card dealt to the Black row will *not* be of the same color as the winning row. In the previous example, *Inverse* would win if the first card dealt to Black were a Diamond and Black won.

When Red and Black each has the same total of 32 points or higher, the hand is a tie, known here as *après*, and nobody wins or loses. If the rows are tied at 31, called *un après*, the bets are impounded—an *en prison* feature like that of European Roulette (see page 47)—and are settled on the next deal.

Casinos that offer *partage* in Roulette also make it available in Trente-et-Quarante. A player who wishes to avoid the *en prison* routine after an *un après* tie at 31–31 may do so, recovering half the original bet at once.

Aside from *un après*, Trente-et-Quarante is a dead-even game. The house vig derives entirely from *en prison* and *partage* at 31–31, and is said to be 1.1 or 1.25 percent, depending on whose probability mathematics you prefer.

An insurance feature permits a slight reduction in this low percentage. Players who pay a fee of 1 percent of their bets are insured against *un après*, recovering their money (but not the fee) when 31–31 ties occur. The fees are returned to the insured after other ties but are collected after each winning or losing deal. In effect, this makes Trente-et-Quarante an absolutely even game for which the gambler pays a fee of 1 percent.

The *tailleur* customarily announces the results in terms of what happened to bets on Red and Color:

1. *Rouge gagne et Couleur*: Red and Color win.
2. *Rouge gagne, Couleur perd*: Red wins, Color loses.
3. *Rouge perd, Couleur gagne*: Red loses, Color wins.
4. *Rouge perd et Couleur*: Red and Color lose.

It is all very civilized and simple and a marvelous means of exercising a favorite betting scheme.

NINE:

FOR
PIGEONS
ONLY

ALTHOUGH I DEPLORE KENO, SLOT MACHINES, AND THE proposition bets at Craps and urge the reader to give them a wide berth, I can understand why the tourist might find them attractive. In this chapter, we shall deal with casino games that lack redeeming features of *any* kind and serve only to separate the improvident from their money.

MONEY WHEELS

Whether known as Big Six or Money Wheel or even Wheel of Fortune, this is a chromium-plated version of the carnival wheels that have fleeced generations of rubes. The dealer spins the huge vertical wheel by hand and, just as in a dozen televised game shows, it finally comes to rest, a suspended leather flapper showing which of the 54 (sometimes 48 or 50) spaces is in the twelve-o'clock position. Sometimes the spaces are decorated with and identified by three-dice patterns, sometimes with dollar amounts, sometimes with the names of horses, sometimes with simple numerals. The house edge ranges between 15 and 25 percent. Why would any sane human being prefer this to Roulette?

BOULE

This outrage is found in the lobbies of French casinos. A sizable rubber ball hurtles around a wooden bowl and lands in one of 18 concavities, each marked with a number from 1 through 9 (two positions per number). The even-money bets are like those of Roulette: *Rouge* wins with 2, 4, 7, or 9; *Noir* with 1, 3, 6, or 8. And a 5 wins for the house. *Pair* wins for the even numbers, *Impair* for the odd, and 5 still wins for the house. *Passe* wins on 6, 7, 8, or 9, and *Manque* wins on the low 1, 2, 3, 4, with 5 again winning for the house. A winning bet *En Plein* on a single number pays at odds of 7–1. All others fetch even money. The house advantage is 11.1 percent on all bets. And this goes on within yards of European Roulette tables.

POKER

Persons with even the slightest knowledge of Poker are aware that it is primarily a game of skill and should never be played with strangers. And of all strangers to avoid, those found at casino Poker tables surely head the list. The casinos have the tables mainly as an accommodation to well-heeled customers, taking a percentage of each pot or charging by the hour, which amounts to the same thing. Some sharks profess to make their livings at these tables and at others in the Poker emporiums of Gardena, California, and I would not be surprised. The quality of their play is leagues beyond that of the Friday-night bloodbath at the kitchen table back home.

Presumably, most recreational gamblers travel all the way to casinos to enjoy forms of recreation unobtainable at home. Let that be reason enough to concentrate on games of pure chance, detouring the Poker. If additional argument be required to convince the reader who happens to be an excellent Poker player, I am told that nobody can make money at casino Poker when playing against worthy opponents. The house takes just enough of the money to absorb the profit. Therefore, those who actually make money at those tables do so by plucking pigeons. I would rather push quarters into a slot machine.

APPENDIX A:

ADDITIONAL READING

As promised, this book has reviewed the sparse principles and simple procedures of expert play at casino gaming tables. The reader may now feel ready for more profound discussion of the games and the probabilities that govern them. Many excellent books supply that information. The newer ones are sometimes available in good bookstores. Older ones may be located in libraries. The best source is the huge mail-order catalogue of Gambler's Book Club, 630 South 11th Street, Box 4115, Las Vegas, Nevada 89106.

I recommend these:

The Science of Chance, by Horace C. Levinson, Ph.D., Rinehart & Co., New York, 1950. This is the clearest and most graceful explanation of probability theory and mathematics ever written for the general public. It is difficult to find, but worth the effort. Includes a great deal about casino gambling.

The Casino Gambler's Guide, by Allan N. Wilson, Harper & Row, New York, 1965. A gambling mathematician's thorough review of the principal games.

Scarne's Guide to Casino Gambling, by John Scarne, Simon & Schuster, New York, 1978. Scarne is a magician who gained wide acclaim during World War II when he toured service installations teaching the troops how to avoid being cheated at games. Since then, he has been a casino overseer and rules-maker and, through his writings, the most prominent of all gambling authorities. This finds him, as usual, unburdened by false modesty. But his expertise is seldom subject to question and he leaves no subject untouched.

Understanding Gambling Systems, by Dean Wiley, Gambler's Book Club Press, Las Vegas, 1975. A neat booklet which establishes a theoretical basis for evaluating systems and then illustrates each system with apt examples.

Casino & Sports, a more-or-less bimonthly magazine published by Gambler's Book Club Press. Investigates and exposes fraudulent mail-order systems, tells what is new in casino procedures, answers readers' questions about tactics, percentages, and other matters of sophisticated interest. Also covers sports betting other than horse racing.

APPENDIX B:

PRACTICE YOUR TECHNIQUE— FOR FREE

THE ESSENCE OF CASINO GAMBLING IS THE BET ON A RAN-
dom occurrence. The casino itself is relevant only as a set-
ting in which such bets can be made. The gilded ceilings,
urbane croupiers, toothsome waitresses, hysterical plungers,
rattling chips, bouncing balls, and snapping cards are
merely atmospheric. What really counts about any true
casino game could be incorporated into a simple slot machine. Indeed, successful casino play depends largely on
one's ability to shut off the atmosphere and its distractions
and concentrate on the bets as if playing a private slot
machine. Putting it differently, the proper time to enjoy
the casino ambience is before and after gambling. Not
during.

The pages that follow should prepare the reader for
successful play. They contain tables of random numbers
that reflect the actual probabilities of, respectively, Craps,
American Roulette, European Roulette, and Baccarat.
Without stretching the imagination beyond reasonable limits, the reader can employ these tables at home in dress

rehearsal for the real thing. Test your favorite systems. Practice whatever mental arithmetic you may plan to employ in actual casino play. Keep track of imaginary wins and losses. Learn to concentrate. A few short sessions here will sharpen your abilities without costing a cent.

The tables of random numbers are reproduced with the generous permission of Dr. William L. Quirin, associate professor of mathematics (computer sciences), Adelphi University, Garden City, New York. A leading investigator of the probabilities of thoroughbred racing, in which his own computer studies are unmatched, Dr. Quirin programmed each game into his machine and produced these numbers for us. Have fun with them.

CRAPS

The following 1,000 numbers occur in a distribution faithful to the probabilities of Craps. By changing their order, you can simulate many thousands of plays while remaining within the real limits of the game. For example, you can take each column in order from top to bottom. Next time, take each row in order from left to right. After that, try each column in order from bottom to top, or alternate columns, or alternate rows, or every other number from back to front.

I have deliberately refrained from displaying anything but the total number produced by each computer-simulated roll of two dice. This means that the reader must confine practice to dry-run bets on Pass, Don't Pass, Free Odds, Come, Don't Come, and other reasonable chances. If you want to practice Hardway betting, you simply did not absorb the material in our chapter on Craps and should go stand in the corner.

[SEE TABLES ON FOLLOWING PAGES.]

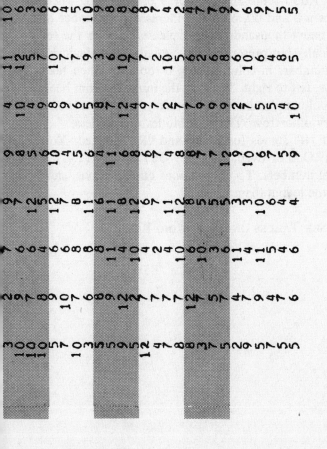

AMERICAN ROULETTE

Here are 1,000 representative turns of a 38-slot wheel that includes a 0 and 00. You can increase the number of turns to as many thousands as you please, varying the sequence radically but preserving the probabilities. Begin by taking the numbers in columns, top to bottom. Then take them in rows, left to right. Then try the numbers from back to front in columns or in rows. Or take every other number, or every other row. The possibilities are endless.

Note that "B" stands for Black and "R" for Red. You also can play Odd or Even, High (19–36) or Low (1–18), or individual numbers. To play various combinations, simply consult the layout diagram.

[SEE TABLES ON FOLLOWING PAGES.]

EUROPEAN ROULETTE

Now for the wheel with a single 0. The charted numbers can be taken in any order, supplying many thousands of plausible sequences which demonstrate the many variations supplied by the long-range probabilities of the game. To test street bets and other combinations, keep an eye on the layout diagram. When trying the even-money bets, such as Red and Black, Odd and Even, High and Low, do not forget the *en prison* feature discussed in our Roulette chapter.

[SEE TABLES ON FOLLOWING PAGES.]

10B	17B	31B	7R	11R	4B	14R	32R	34R	13B
22B	5R	15R	0	25R	33B	33B	20B	10R	28B
35B	12R	10B	30B	23B	10B	34B	35B	19R	24B
36R	32R	6B	19R	15B	31B	19R	19B	1	20R
3R	26B	33B	32R	21R	10B	5R	25R	1B	16R
34R	4B	34R	36R	20R	4B	9R	0	24B	1R
24B	22B	5B	8R	25R	36R	32R	30B	37R	18R
33B	14R	6B	21R	23R	25R	29B	32B	15B	21R
24B	9B	13R	24R	17B	3B	26B	4B	19R	8B
13B	27R	16R	9R	18R	27R	28B	23R	34R	5R
11B	9R	36R	33B	10B	28B	27R	24R	21R	11B
13B	14R	27R	24B	20R	5R	21R	7R	16R	9R
16B	29R	34R	26B	23R	17B	31B	21R	15R	33R
28B	12R	8B	24B	29B	25R	21B	23R	35B	18R
25R	13B	23R	20B	21B	36B	14R	2R	45R	32R
20R	28B	7R	3R	10R	29R	26B	18R	20R	15R
21B	24R	4B	8B	3R	36R	33B	17B	7R	19B
27R	14R	30R	7R	7R	23R	29B	26B	35B	28B
23R	27R	25R	19R	29B	7R	32R	29R	34R	21B
24B	5R	23R	24B	35B	20B	30R	21R		6B
6B	33B	10B	14R		10B		0		29B
5R	16R	12B							36R
	36R								

BACCARAT

"B" stands for a win by the Banker hand, "P" is a win for the Player hand. No ties are shown, because ties are irrelevant.

[SEE TABLES ON FOLLOWING PAGES.]

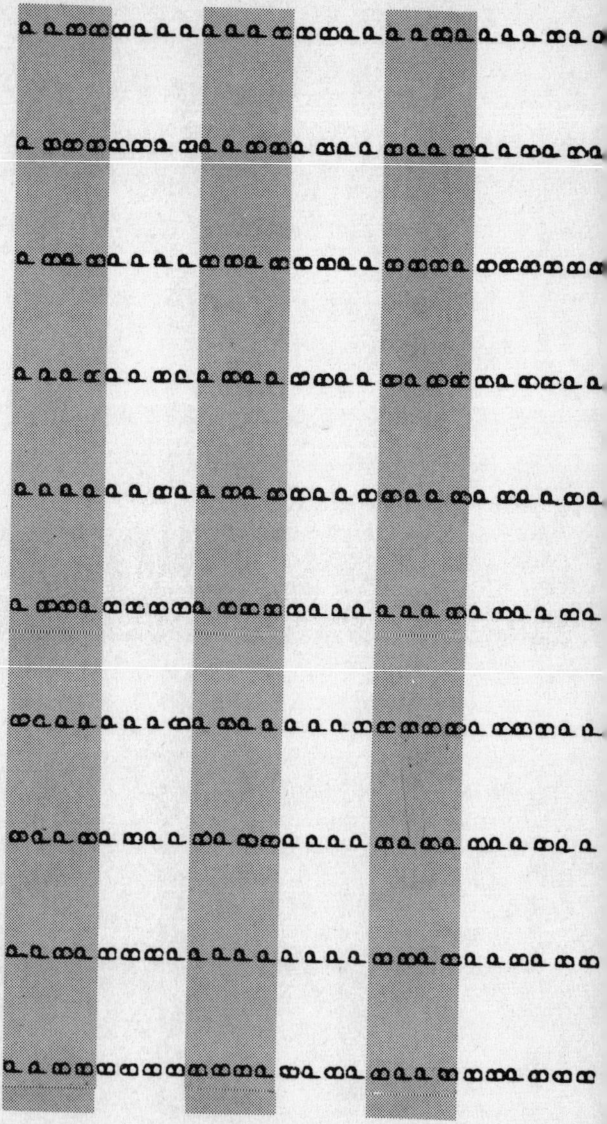

CASINO
GLOSSARY

ACE. Card that counts 1 or 11 in *Blackjack*, 1 in *Baccarat*; die showing one spot; one dollar.

A CHEVAL. *European Roulette*: A split bet on two numbers.

ACTION. Betting activity.

ACTIVE PLAYER. *Chemin de Fer*: Whoever bets most on Player hand is dealt the cards and has some options on whether to draw.

ADA FROM DECATUR. *Craps*: An 8.

ANCHOR MAN. *Blackjack*: Player seated at Third Base, to extreme right of dealer, is last to play before dealer and may benefit from seeing cards exposed by others.

ASSOCIÉ. In *Baccarat*, a standee who bets as the Banker's partner, not widely permitted in America.

AUCTION. *Chemin de Fer*: Bidding to determine who shall be Banker.

AVEC. *Chemin de Fer*: Also *avec la table,* an offer by a player to cover half the Banker's bet.

BACK LINE. *Craps*: The Don't Pass area of the layout. Thus, a *back-line player* and *back-line odds.*

BANCO. *Chemin de Fer*: A player's bid to cover the Banker's entire bet.

BANCO SUIVI. *Chemin de Fer*: Having called "Banco" and lost, the same player now asserts priority to cover the Banker's entire bet again.

BANK. The casino's funds.

BANK CRAPS. The casino dice game, which differs from private Craps in that players bet against the house rather than against each other.

BANKER. *Baccarat*: One of the two hands, which, in Chemin de Fer, is actually banked by one of the players rather than the casino management.

BANQUIER. See Banker.

BAR. *Craps*: "Except," as in "Don't Pass Bar 2," which means that a bet on Don't Pass neither wins nor loses if a 2 turns up.

BIG DICK. *Craps*: A 10.

BIG EIGHT. *Craps*: A proposition bet with its own layout space in which players wager that an 8 will precede the next 7. The same bet can be made as a Place bet with a lower house percentage.

BIG ONE. One thousand dollars; "a grand."

BIX SIX. *Craps*: An alternative to Big Eight and no better.

BLACK. *Roulette*: One of the even-money bets; *Noir*.

BLACKJACK. A count of 21 in two cards—an Ace and a 10 or picture card. Wins unless the dealer also draws one.

BOARD. *Craps*: The inner wall or "rail" of the table against which shooter must throw the dice.

BOXMAN. *Craps*: Casino functionary who runs table.

BOX NUMBERS. *Craps*: 4, 5, 6, 8, 9, and 10 each has its own display on the layout. The dealer marks the shooter's point by placing the puck in the proper box. Place bets also go into those boxes.

BREAK. *Blackjack*: A bust hand of 22 points or more.

BUCK. *Craps*: The puck with which dealer marks the shooter's point.

BUY BET. *Craps*: To get correct odds on a Place bet, the player pays a commission, making it a Buy but no bargain.

CAP. *Craps and Roulette*: Disapproved practice of dealer putting winning chips atop the original bet rather than alongside.

CARRÉ. *European Roulette*: A Corner bet on four numbers.

CARTE. In European *Baccarat,* a request that a card be dealt.

CASE. *Blackjack*: To watch the deals, counting the exposed cards to keep track of deck's changing composition: a "casedowner" is a card counter of that kind.

CASINO MANAGER. The person in charge of the entire place.

CHANCE. The probabilities, expressed as a percentage (.33), an equivalent fraction (⅓), or equivalent odds (2–1).

CHECK. A chip.

CHOP. A pattern of outcomes in which no prolonged streaks occur, such as alternating Reds and Blacks or Passes and Don't Passes.

COLONNE. *European Roulette*: A column bet on 12 numbers.

COLUMN BET. *Roulette*: A bet on one of the three columns of 12 numbers; *European Roulette*: Colonne.

COMBINATION. *Keno*: A ticket calling for elaborate combinations of numbers and ways.

COME BET. *Craps*: Regarding the next roll as a come out, a bet that the result will be a Pass.

COME OUT. *Craps*: After a pass or a seven-out, the first roll.

COME-OUT BET. *Craps*: A bet whose outcome depends on the next roll; Hop bet.

COMMISSION. *Baccarat*: House deduction from winnings on Banker hand. *Craps*: House deduction from Buy bets.

CORNER BET. *Roulette*: A bet on four numbers; square bet or quarter bet.

COUP. *Roulette* and *Baccarat*: A round of play as represented by one winning or losing outcome.

CRAPOUT. *Craps*: A 2, 3, or 12 on the first roll.

CROUPIER. Dealer in Roulette or Baccarat.

CURATOR. *Baccarat*: In British versions, the player who performs rituals as Banker without actually banking the bets.

CUT. Final formality of placing top of pack on bottom after shuffle and before dealing; house commission.

DEUCE. In cards or dice, a 2.

DON'T-COME BET. *Craps*: Regarding next roll as come out, a bet on Don't Pass.

DON'T-PASS BET. *Craps*: A bet that the shooter will produce a 2, 3, or 12 on the first roll or, having rolled a point, will produce a 7 before repeating the point.

DOUBLE DOWN. *Blackjack*: Player doubles bet after seeing first two cards, and gets only one additional card.

DOZEN. *Roulette*: A bet on 1 to 12, 13 to 24, or 25 to 36, spaces for each of which are marked on the table layout. *European Roulette*: Douzaine.

DRAG DOWN. Having won, to remove all or part of the profits and let the remainder ride on the next bet.

EN PLEIN. *European Roulette*: A bet on a single number.

EN PRISON. *European Roulette*: When 0 turns up, chips wagered on any of the even-money possibilities are impounded and their disposition is determined by the next turn of the wheel. If the hoped-for outcome occurs, the player gets the money back. Otherwise the house keeps it.

EVEN. *Roulette*: A bet that the next number will be an even one. *European Roulette*: Pair.

FACE CARD. A picture card.

FAITES VOS JEUX. In European casinos, the croupier's request that bets be made.

FIELD. *Craps*: Part of the layout displays 2, 3, 4, 9, 10, 11, and 12 (in some places the 5 instead of 9). A Field bet wins if one of the numbers appears on the next roll.

FIRST BASE. *Blackjack*: Player seated at the dealer's extreme left, first to be dealt cards and first to play the hand.

FIRST DOZEN. *Roulette*: Bet on numbers 1–12.

FIVE-NUMBER BET. *Roulette*: On 0, 00, 1, 2, and 3.

FLOOR MAN. Casino supervisor who works as roving troubleshooter.

FOUR-NUMBER BET. *Roulette*: Corner bet.

FREE ODDS. *Craps*: After shooter establishes the point, a Pass or Come bettor may make an additional bet which pays true odds if it wins, or a Don't Pass or Don't Come bettor may lay such odds against the house. Some places offer so-called double odds, which means that the additional bet may be twice as large as the original.

FRET. Partition between the numbered compartments in a Roulette wheel.

218

FRONT LINE. *Craps*: The layout area where Pass bets are placed.

HARDWAY. *Craps*: A bet that the shooter will roll a specific even number with each die showing the same number of pips (2–2, 3–3, 4–4, or 5–5) before rolling that number another way or throwing a 7.

HIGH. *Roulette*: A bet that the next turn will produce a number between 19 and 36 inclusive. *European Roulette*: Passe.

HIGH ROLLER. Big bettor.

HIT. *Blackjack*: Draw a card. *Craps*: Win.

HOP. *Craps*: Any bet on the outcome of the next roll.

HORN. *Craps*: A combination Hop bet in which the gambler wins if the 2, 3, 11, or 12 appears on the next roll.

HUIT. In European *Baccarat*, eight.

IMPAIR. *European Roulette*: A bet on Odd.

INSIDE BETS. *Roulette*: Bets placed on or among the numbers themselves rather than on the Red, Black, Odd, Even, High, Low, and Column areas outside that part of the table layout.

INSURANCE. *Blackjack*: When dealer's exposed card is an Ace, players are invited to bet that the house hand will be a Blackjack.

LAY BET. *Craps*: If a player has not bet on Don't Pass, some casinos permit the player to lay true odds against the shooter's point by paying a 5 percent commission.

LAY ODDS. *Craps*: A free-odds bet by a back-line player.

LAYOUT. The table diagram on which bettors and dealers place chips in spaces marked for the various types of bets.

LET RIDE. Having won a bet, to leave all proceeds in place for a new bet on the same terms.

LIMIT. The largest bet accepted at a table.

LINE BET. *Roulette*: A six-number bet on two adjoining streets. *European Roulette*: Sixaine.

LITTLE JOE. "Little Joe from Kokomo"; *Craps*: A 4.

LONG HAND. *Craps*: When many rolls are made before a decision after the come out.

LOW. *Roulette*: A bet that the next number will be anything from 1 through 18. *European Roulette*: Manque.

MANQUE. *European Roulette*: Low.

MARTINGALE. A betting system in which the size of the bet is increased (usually doubled) after each loss.

MAXIMUM. The house or table limit on bet size.

MIDDLE DOZEN. *Roulette*: A bet on the middle column of 12 numbers.

MINIMUM. The smallest bet accepted at a table.

NATURAL.   *Baccarat*: An 8 or 9 in two cards. *Blackjack*: 21 in two cards. *Craps*: A 7 or 11 on the first roll.

NEIGHBORS.   *Roulette*: Numbers close to each other on the wheel.

NEUF.   In European *Baccarat*, nine.

NINETY DAYS.   *Craps*: A 9.

NO DICE.   *Craps*: When a roll does not count because dice were improperly thrown or did not finish flat on the table.

NOIR.   *European Roulette*: Black.

NON.   European *Baccarat*: "No," meaning that no third card is wanted.

ODD.   *Roulette*: A bet that the next spin will produce an odd number. *European Roulette*: Impair.

ODDS.   The ratio between winnings and the amount bet. Thus, 2–1 means winnings of two units for each unit wagered.

ONE-ROLL BET.   *Craps*: A bet on the outcome of the next roll; Hop bet.

OUTSIDE.   *Roulette*: Bets placed on any part of the table diagram outside the boxes that display the 37 or 38 numbers.

PAIR.   *European Roulette*: Even.

PAROLI.   A parlay in which the player lets the proceeds of a winning bet ride on the next round of play.

PASS. *Craps*: When the dice win for the shooter.

PASS LINE. *Craps*: The front line, where Pass bets are placed.

PASSE. *European Roulette*: High (19 through 36).

PERCENTAGE. The house advantage, expressed as the percentage of wagered money it can expect to retain on a particular bet or game; edge, vigorish, vig.

PIT BOSS. Casino functionary in charge of a table or group of tables.

POINT. *Craps*: When a 4, 5, 6, 8, 9, or 10 is rolled on the come out, it becomes the shooter's point.

PRESS. Increase the size of one's bets.

PROGRESSION. A betting procedure in which the amount bet increases after each loss.

PROPOSITION. The terms of a bet. *Craps*: A bet other than the usual Pass, Don't Pass, etc., usually at high odds with a high house percentage.

PUNTER. *Baccarat*: A player, especially one who bets against the bank.

PUSH. A tie or standoff.

RED. *Roulette*: A bet that the next number will be red. *European Roulette*: Rouge.

RIEN NE VA PLUS. French croupier's announcement that no more bets will be accepted on the upcoming play.

RIGHT BETTOR. *Craps*: One who bets on Pass; front-line bettor.

ROUGE. *European Roulette*: Red.

SABOT. In Europe, a dealing shoe.

SAWDUST JOINT. An unglamorous casino with low minimums.

SEVEN OUT. *Craps*: Lose by rolling a 7 before making one's point.

SHOE. A box from which cards are dealt.

SHOOTER. *Craps*: The player who rolls the dice.

SIXAINE. *European Roulette*: A six-number bet on two adjoining streets; a line bet.

SNAKE EYES. *Craps*: A 2.

SPLIT. *Roulette*: A bet on two adjoining numbers.

SPLITTING PAIRS. *Blackjack*: When dealt two cards of the same denomination, the player may separate them, double the original bet, and use each as the beginning of a new hand.

SPOT. *Keno*: A bet on an individual number or numbers but not on combinations thereof.

SQUARE. *Roulette*: A bet on four numbers; corner bet; quarter bet; Carré.

STANDOFF. A tie or push in which neither the player nor the house wins the chips.

STICKMAN. Casino employee who manages the dice at a

Craps table, pushing them with a long-handled stick to the shooter and calling the results of each roll.

STIFF HAND. *Blackjack*: A two-card total of 12 to 16, susceptible to break on the next card.

STRAIGHT. *Roulette*: A bet on a single number. *European Roulette*: En Plein.

STREET. *Roulette*: A bet on a row of three numbers. *European Roulette*: Transversale Plein.

TAKE ODDS. *Craps*: When a Pass or Come bettor supplements the bet with a wager at the true odds against the shooter's point.

THIRD BASE. *Blackjack*: The seat at the dealer's extreme right.

TOKE. A tip given to casino employee or entire table crew by appreciative gambler.

TRANSVERSALE PLEIN. *European Roulette*: A three-number street bet.

TWENTY-ONE. Blackjack.

VIGORISH. The house percentage; vig.

WAY BET. *Keno*: A ticket marked to register bets on numbers combined in various ways.

WRONG BETTOR. *Craps*: A Don't Pass bettor who wins when the dice lose; back-line bettor.